Going Forth

Going Forth

Women's Leadership Issues in Higher Education and Physical Education

BY

MARY J. HOFEREK

PRINCETON BOOK COMPANY, PUBLISHERS

PRINCETON, NEW JERSEY

Library of Congress Catalog Card Number 85–060704
ISBN 916622–40–1
Printed in the United States of America

Design by Bruce Campbell Design
Cover Design by Design & Illustration
Typography by TypeHouse of Pennington

Contents

Introduction. 1
1 What Is Leadership? 3
2 Leadership and Cultural Expectations 10
3 Overt and Covert Curriculum. 20
4 Women As Faculty and Professionals 30
5 Overcoming Gates and Hurdles 44
6 Environments Fostering Success. 54
7 Going Forth. 68
References 70
Organizations 77
Index. 80

Introduction

Going Forth was born in the struggle for women to take their rightful place in higher education. In the past, women were systematically and deliberately denied full access to higher education. While a relatively small number of woman were educated in the 1800's, the proportion of women in higher education has increased markedly since then (Lerner, 1983). In the 1980's women are a numerical majority of undergraduates in many institutions. A statistical majority in student enrollment, however, does not ensure equality of educational opportunity. *Going Forth* assesses and explores the place of women in higher education in relation to their potential for leadership. The book specifically examines women in physical education, athletics, and recreation, but is applicable to all women in higher education.

Regardless of their role as student, faculty, or staff, women collectively remain on the margin. The distribution of women on faculties indicates that they are clustered in the lowest ranks from which they rarely move; staffing patterns demonstrate similar trends. Besides the demographic patterns, analytic studies on salary equity and decision-making positions held by women show that women have little power in institutions of higher learning.

Moving from the margin to the center of these institutions is the challenge. The groundwork for moving forward has already been laid through the scholarship and written records of women before this generation. Unlike women who did not know the work done by those before them and therefore repeated over and over again major tasks, women in education today have a heritage that can serve as a foundation for future efforts (Lerner, 1983).

As women are struggling toward the core, the essence of educational institutions is being scrutinized. What is really taught is being questioned. For example, with the exception of women's studies, most college curricula focus on men and men's issues. Books written by males are the basic texts for female students. Researchers are exploring how the "hidden curriculum" in schools affects the self-vision female students develop. The presence or absence of role models, focus on women's issues, and teacher expectations for high performance by women are only some of the variables in educational settings that shape a vision of what is possible.

The true outcomes of the education process are being reevaluated. For example, full-time college enrollment has been found to be advantageous for men but disadvantageous for women as measured by increases in confidence and career commitment (Stake, 1984), a finding in contrast to the stated objectives of most educational institutions. Furthermore, many educators believe their mission is to develop the full potential of each student. Unless women can be brought to the center, however, maximum potential will only be developed in less than 50 percent of the student population. To develop full potential for women as well as men, the structure of educational environments will have to be changed. Common obstacles and barriers for women, such as job segregation, exclusion, and salary inequity, are pervasive in institutions throughout the country. The "club"-like atmosphere of the professions, lack of mentors, and blatant discrimination continue to diminish opportunities for women.

Strategies to overcome the barriers are being developed—women's networks, a hard confrontation with minority-group self-hatred and methods to overcome it, solid research on institutional environments—these are promising developments for what some have called the revolution in education. It is a complex task that requires collective action.

Even as educational institutions have received close scrutiny, women and some men have also examined the concept of leadership itself. The "messiah" theory of one leader who is expected to save everyone is not relevant for human leaders in a highly intricate, technological society. Styles of leadership that worked well in the past will not necessarily work in the future. Alternatives are being explored by women's groups and may contribute to our knowledge of leadership behavior.

Within the female 51 percent of our society are the leaders of tomorrow. For our educational future and the future of education, a serious scholarly effort must be made to clarify the issues, synthesize the relevant research, and explore the options of leadership. *Going Forth* is meant to be the beginning of this effort as women move toward the center of higher-education institutions.

1

What Is Leadership?

Leadership is a term that is frequently used but rarely agreed upon. As challenges to leadership behaviors have been made, a closer scrutiny of what leadership really means has been undertaken. While traditional definitions are still used, creative thinkers are reconceptualizing and redefining the term.

Some researchers have used general definitions; for example, Athos and Coffey (1968): "A leader is one who influences his followers to achieve an objective in a given situation." Both formal and informal leadership are included. Formal leaders, commonly called managers, have authority and status due to their position in the system. Managers have the right to direct or command people in order to achieve objectives. Informal leaders may not have a formal organizational position; they exert leadership by influencing others through personal power or informal authority to achieve objectives. Given these definitions, effective managers usually are leaders as well as managers.

There are those who define leadership by seeking to identify people who are leaders:

> . . . assigned to the leader role . . . , either with or without the enumeration of special duties and functions.
> . . . identified as such by observers, or by group members, either with or without the delineation of criteria for identification.
> . . . whose presence and/or behaviors in the group strongly influence the group's activities or products.
> . . . who are highly chosen by other members as friends, confidants, or co-workers.
> . . . whose suggestions, commands, or example are regularly accepted and followed by other group members.
> . . . who occupy certain positions within an institutionalized

> role structure—foremen, lieutenants, company presidents.
> . . . with whom others identify, and who therefore inspire and channel the activities of group members.
> . . . who are observed to perform certain specified functions [such as fund raising] (Steiner, 1972).

Others have discussed the leadership role or the functions leaders serve. Krech and others (Loy, McPherson, & Kenyon, 1978) acknowledge the complexity of the role and state that a leader must serve as: "1) executive, 2) planner, 3) policymaker, 4) expert, 5) external group representative, 6) controller of internal relations, 7) purveyor of rewards and punishments, 8) exemplar, 9) symbol of the group, 10) substitute for individual responsibility, 11) ideologist, 12) father figure, and 13) scapegoat." The first seven functions are viewed as primary, the others are accessory.

Another functional position is based on the instrumental and/or emotional needs of the group. From this perspective, it has been noted that groups frequently have one individual who helps to clarify group goals and then works instrumentally toward the achievement of the specified tasks. The instrumental leader keeps the group on track and prods it forward. On the other hand, the emotional leader takes care of the social or feeling aspects of the group: interpersonal conflicts are resolved, ruffled feelings are soothed, and group morale is boosted. Proponents of this dualistic perspective argue that both kinds of leaders are needed.

Some writers have concluded that a definition of leadership must go beyond an attempt to focus on one person. They believe that many variables interact to shape the leadership situation. Athos and Coffey (1968) contend that "effective leadership depends on the leader, his followers, the situation, and the interrelationships between them. Leadership is one element in a social system." The situation makes the leader and the leader makes the situation.

Thus, definitions of leadership range broadly from the individual to the system. The literature reveals that we are moving from static, simplistic notions of leadership to dynamic, deeply complex, multivariate concepts.

Leadership Development

A better understanding of how one becomes a leader is also developing. At one time, researchers felt that there was an ideal leadership personality. The approach to leadership research, therefore, involved finding persons who were acknowledged leaders and testing them to find common personality characteristics. However, no one personality pattern could be found for an ideal leader for every situation.

The approach that is emerging involves a consideration of both the person and the situation (Denmark, 1977)—different situations require leaders with diverse abilities and skills at various times. Furthermore, leadership is dependent not only on the person's potential, but on the vision each person has of herself or himself as well as the availability of opportunities to learn the necessary skills for effective leadership.

According to what some call social-learning theory (Mischel, 1975), one way people learn how they should behave is by observing models, actual or portrayed models, like themselves. If women observe other women in the activity professions exerting leadership by chairing departments, conducting high-level research, publishing articles, testifying at Congressional hearings, writing books, serving on advisory boards, participating in policy-making bodies like the United States Olympic Committee (USOC), or advising neophyte professionals, these women are more likely to visualize themselves as capable of and interested in performing the same tasks. Therefore, the vision each woman develops of herself as a professional in the discipline is related to what she sees other women doing in the field (Hoferek, 1980a).

Social-learning theory implies that negative learning about women can occur as well. If no women are present in high-level positions, the absence of models would suggest that those positions are for men only. The denigration of women through sexist jokes or other demeaning actions would also produce negative learning by indicating to women that they are second-class citizens in the profession.

The same method of learning operates for racial/ethnic minorities in the profession: blacks in leadership positions are role models for other blacks, and Hispanics in leadership positions are role models for other Hispanics, and so forth. Thus, the presence or absence of and the respectful or disrespectful treatment of racial/ethnic minorities in the profession affects the vision each racial/ethnic-minority person develops of herself or himself.

The need for opportunities to learn leadership skills is also being recognized. Strategies that have been suggested to enhance leadership by women include in-service workshops to deal with discriminatory practices and attitudes, leadership training institutes, national identification programs for potential leaders, awards for research on leadership issues for women, internship programs, and strong recruitment efforts (Hoferek, 1980a).

Leadership Styles

The concept of leadership style—how one acts in the role—has been evolving even as leadership itself has been reconceptualized. Traditional leadership styles are usually described as autocratic (or authoritarian), democratic (consultive), or laissez-faire (free-rein). The authoritarian is described as one who uses formal authority, rewards, and punishments to get obedience. Decision-making and policy development rest solely in the person of the authoritarian. The democratic leader encourages participation and may allow the group considerable input into policy decisions and even the opportunity to set policy. The laissez-faire leader exerts minimal control and acts primarily as a resource to facilitate group accomplishment (Athos & Coffey, 1968).

While many leaders may use one style most of the time, a particular leader may use all three at various times. It may be more effective, for example, for a primarily democratic leader to be authoritarian in a crisis situation in which lives are at stake. Thus, the situation as well as the leader and followers may determine which style is most effective (Athos & Coffey, 1968).

As women became more aware of their potential for leadership through the Women's Liberation Movement, they not only wanted access to more decision-making positions, but questioned the styles being used by men. During the 1960's and even the

1970's, much of the leadership literature, with its male pronouns and male authors, seemed to be written about and for men. Therefore, for many women, the challenge was not only to get a top-level position but to conceptualize leadership alternatives that would reflect the values and potential of women in general. Several options emerged from the creative work of women and women's groups.

Those who focused on one person as a leader found an alternative style in the androgyny model developed by Bem (1974). When applied to leadership, the androgyny framework provides for individuals who balance instrumentality and expressiveness. Rather than the image of the strictly instrumental manager who is hard-driving, competitive, and unemotional, this model maintains that qualities in the expressive cluster, such as sensitivity, gentleness, and compassion, enhance leadership. Thus, if difficult decisions, such as firing an employee, are to be made, the androgynous leader considers and deals with the emotional impact. Although the "androgynous advantage" in management has not been proven, it is an option that has emerged from research by women.

Two other alternatives deal directly with group decision-making rather than one-person leadership. Consensual decision-making and shared leadership have evolved as styles used by women's groups. While the two can overlap in reality, they will be discussed separately.

Consensual decision-making usually includes discussion until everyone can agree. This decision-making style was illustrated by Gearhart in her book, *The Wanderground* (1978). During the meeting described as the "gatherstretch," an issue was discussed and many women contributed their feelings and beliefs. Action would be taken on the issue if a "clear wish" could be reached by the group or if consensus occurred.

There are advantages and disadvantages to consensual decision-making. Because all viewpoints are discussed and everyone must agree, the process may take much longer than the majority-rule process or authoritarian edict. Furthermore, one person can block what may be beneficial to the entire group. There may also be considerable pressure to conform, and the process may be faulted by the "group think" phenomenon—the lone dissenter gives in even though she or he is the only one who is right.* (The Bay of Pigs catastrophy was attributed to a "group think" problem.) In Gearhart's (1978) illustration, the conformity problem was overcome by allowing the dissenter to act on her own as long as she represented and spoke only for herself.

The advantages of consensual decision-making were hinted at in the gatherstretch material presented in *The Wanderground*: The participants were at times frightened by the strength they felt and could potentially unleash. There is power when a group of women have discussed an issue thoroughly and have agreed on a course of action.*

In shared leadership, the sharing may be formal when various people provide leadership in certain areas of inquiry for the group, or informal when different individuals emerge as leaders at unplanned times. In the sharing process, some groups have made concerted efforts to reduce the hierarchies or class structures in the group and thereby to facilitate a full participation model.*

Again, there are advantages and disadvantages to this alternative style. The notion of equal participation rights in groups without hierarchies can cause conflict in a group. If a person with more expertise than anyone else in the group explains at length her position on an issue, she may be seen as monopolizing the group's time and impeding the participation rights of others. For some, the attempt to eliminate hierarchies feels false because it does not represent the "real" world; for example, a graduate student may argue with a professor in a women's group and then attend a class in which the same professor grades her. The advantages of shared leadership are obvious: Good ideas may be voiced by anyone in the group, regardless of status; the act of participating may enhance a member's commitment to the group, and so forth.*

*Succeeding statements in the chapter that are marked with an asterisk are based on the author's experiences in women's groups.

These alternatives constructed by women's groups may anticipate the leadership styles of the future. Toffler in *The Third Wave* (1980) predicts that the "messiahs" of the past will not lead in the future. Since our society has changed, leaders must change and a whole "new type of leadership" will be needed:

> The requisite qualities of Third Wave leaders are not yet entirely clear. We may well find that strength lies not in a leader's assertiveness but precisely in his or her ability to listen to others; not in bulldozer force but in imagination; not in megalomania but in a recognition of the limited nature of leadership in the new world.
>
> The leaders of tomorrow may well have to deal with a far more decentralized and participatory society—one even more diverse than today's. They can never again be all things to all people. Indeed, it is unlikely that one human being will ever embody all the traits required. Leadership may well prove to be more temporary, collegial, and consensual.

One can only imagine what these changes in society and leadership styles will mean for future educators. Can a high participation, consensual model be effective for a teacher in a public school? How can a specific department benefit by shared leadership? How can diverse groups external to the educational institution contribute to, rather than detract from, the schools of tomorrow? What if no one can agree on anything?

No clear answers are readily apparent. If Toffler is right, however, new styles of leadership will be needed by classroom teachers, administrators, boards, and students to meet the challenges of tomorrow.

The conceptualization of the term leadership has been shifting from a focus on seeking the "best" person to one of formulating new styles or forms. Exciting options are emerging that may have the potential for fulfilling the needs of our society in the future.

2

Leadership and Cultural Expectations

Due to popular images about women in our society, there may be a cultural expectation that females do not want to be leaders and, if they do become leaders, are not "good" leaders. This cultural expectation may be due, in part, to the behaviors associated with the sex-role stereotyping of women and the expectation for "feminine" characteristics as defined by traditional standards. Included in the "feminine" cluster of behaviors are characteristics such as weakness, passivity, and dependency (Broverman et al., 1970). Since leadership usually involves the antithesis of feminine behaviors and requires characteristics such as strength, assertion, and independence, the roles of woman and leader may seem incongruous to women themselves and to significant people around them. From such stereotypic perceptions, one may assume that women experience internal role conflict when they find themselves in leadership positions.

Internal Role Conflict

This is based on the widespread belief that women perceive themselves as high on socioemotional or expressive characteristics and low on or lacking instrumental characteristics, that is, women see themselves as possessing high degrees of warmth, gentleness, and sensitivity, but low degrees of decision-making, leadership-behavior, and risk-taking abilities. Therefore, the expectations and requirements in the situation are assumed to be incongruent with the prescriptions for "feminine" women.

In the past, most psychological tests forced people to describe themselves as being on one side or the other of a dichotomy: high socioemotional and low instrumental or low socioemotional and high instrumental (Figure 2-1). Thus, psychometric tests reinforced the common belief that people were either socioemotional or instrumental, but not both. According to this model, women, in

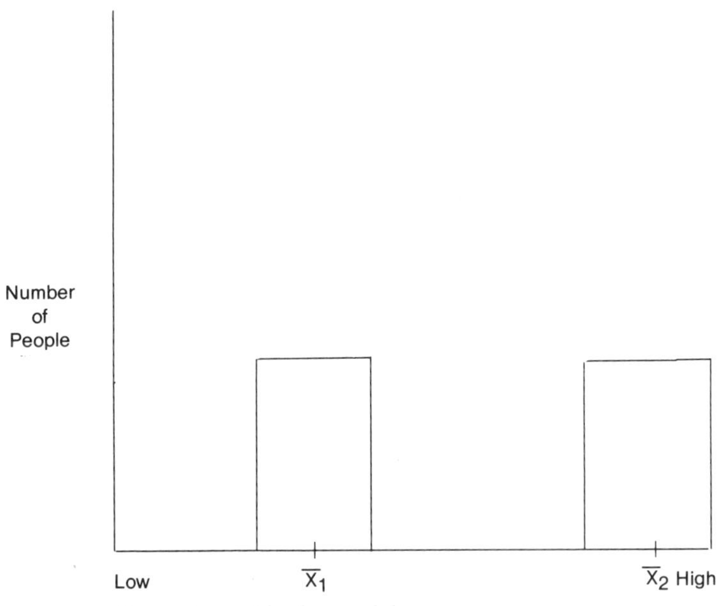

Figure 2-1. Bipolar model.

particular, were socioemotional while men were instrumental. The dichotomy implied by previous psychometric tests has been challenged by Bem (1974) and other researchers (Helreich & Spencer, 1976; Rebecca, Hefner, & Oleshansky, 1976), who say that this notion is simplistic. In reality, people are more complex than the bipolar approach considered. The researchers noted that many people in this country did not "fit" into the dualistic model and that in some cultures in the world, the stereotypes for each sex could not be supported. In fact, in some cultures, the stereotypes seemed to be the opposite.

Essentially, Bem (1974) maintained that some people are balanced in their perceptions of themselves as socioemotional and instrumental (Figure 2-2), and therefore that psychometric instruments and psychological theory should consider people she called androgynous. *Andro* means male and *gyn* means female. Androgyny refers to the perception of oneself as high on socioemotional characteristics *and* high on instrumental characteristics. Thus, the androgyny framework theoretically accounts

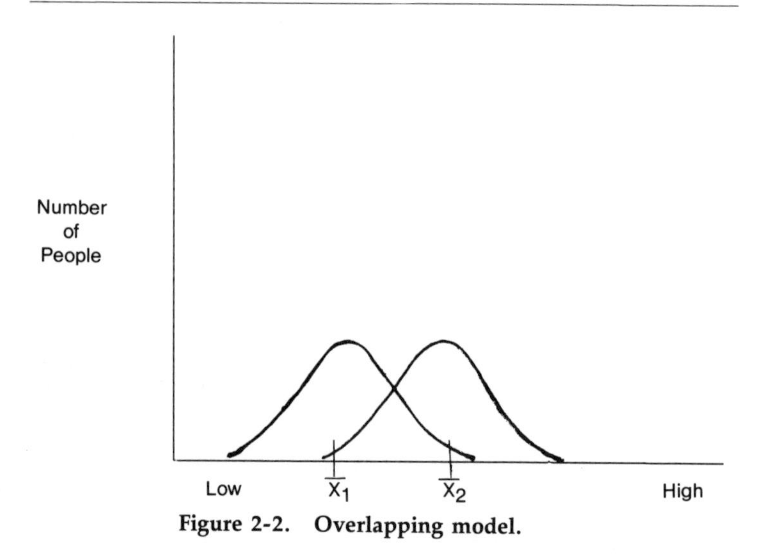

Figure 2-2. Overlapping model.

for the aggressive male football player who gently plays with children in the neighborhood as well as for the female athletic director who makes tough policy decisions in one situation and comforts a losing coach in another situation.

While the androgyny framework has been criticized recently as imposing another prescription or stereotype, it was very important for several reasons. First, Bem (1974) articulated and brought to consciousness dualistic patterns of thinking that were commonly used but were based on unconscious beliefs. Second, the framework provided an alternative way of thinking about the potential of females and males.

People who perceive themselves as highly socioemotional and highly instrumental would not experience internal role conflict in leadership positions because the requirements of the situation would always be consistent with some part of their self-perception. Women in physical education, like women scientists (Helmreich & Spence, 1976), tend to rate themselves high on both clusters of characteristics (Hoferek, 1982) and therefore, theoretically, would be comfortable and competent in leadership positions.

The most effective leaders may be those who, contrary to the assumptions of proponents of internal role conflict, are capable of handling the instrumental demands and the socioemotional demands of the leadership situation. As Heide (1978) has said, "Women who have been taught to care are learning to care enough to be brave; men who have been taught to be brave must learn to be brave enough to care." This is an area for further research and future discussion.

External Role Conflict

While most women in physical education probably do not experience internal role conflict, they may experience external role conflict, which refers to the logistics, such as time commitment and energy, involved in fulfilling the demands of one's professional career and personal life. The traditional resolution of external role conflict for women in the professions may have been to not marry, to drop out after marrying, or to assume the role of married woman in addition to the role of professional woman. The question for many women was how to juggle the competing time demands of career and family.

External role conflict may become more severe when women combine the roles of wife and professional with that of mother. The professional-wife-mother role triad may cause role strain (Hanick, 1981). In addition to being overloaded with time and energy demands, those who choose the three roles may find other areas that produce stress: social norms that may tell the woman to stay home or drop out of the work force, while her personal norms tell her to achieve in the profession; forming and maintaining a supportive social network; potential conflict between the family's stage of formation and the professional's stage of development. In reference to the first stress area, when it is not the norm for women to work, the employed woman may be seen as a threat or a competitor by nonworking women and by some men. There may also be a disruption in the formation of social contacts. For example, dual career families may be more likely to entertain friends acquired by both the wife and the husband rather than just the husband's associates. Conflict in family and professional role cycles may occur. For example, if the couple have children before both careers are established, more stress may be produced (Hanick, 1981).

To deal with external role conflict, several coping devices

have been suggested for professionals who are wives and mothers. Some of these stress-reducing techniques involve setting priorities, compartmentalizing the responsibilities of the various roles so overlap is avoided, and using social structures, such as sharing a law practice with a spouse. Other, more pragmatic suggestions for dealing with external role conflict include part-time work, flexitime jobs, job sharing, freelancing, hiring someone to assist with domestic chores, delegating tasks, associating with other professional women in similar circumstances, choosing social networks that are supportive of working women, and using cooperative neighborhood daycare and meal preparation (Hanick, 1981). Other suggestions, which have been tried in this country, are paternity leaves for fathers of newborn children, paternity days off from work to care for sick children or attend school functions, and company-operated daycare centers that allow children to be near their parents. Other techniques may be developed that reduce the strain usually borne by women who choose to work, to be married, and to have children.

Misperceptions and Myths

The role conflict assumption is not the only misperception professional women have to deal with. In referring to the physical education profession, Duquin (1979) has stated: "The woman who decides to seek leadership status must learn to deal with both the misperceptions of her co-workers and supervisors as regards the proper role of women in organizations." Thus, supervisors and co-workers may have expectations and assumptions about the female professional that are related more to how they see women as a group than to the individual woman's abilities and skills.

COMMON MISPERCEPTIONS AND MYTHS

The Myth	*The Reality*
A woman's place is in the home.	Homemaking in itself is no longer a full-time job for most people. Goods and services formerly produced in the home are now commercially

The Myth	*The Reality*
	available; laborsaving devices have lightened or eliminated much work around the home.[1] Sixty-two percent of all women 18 to 64 years of age were workers in 1981, compared with 91 percent of men. Fifty-two percent of all women 16 years and over were workers. Labor force participation was highest among women ages 20 to 24 (70 percent). About 47 million women were in the labor force in 1981; only 32 million in 1971.[2]
The majority of women are not seriously attached to the labor force; they work only for extra pocket money.	The majority of women work because of economic need. Two-thirds (66 percent) of all women in the labor force in March 1982 were single (25 percent), widowed (5 percent), divorced (11 percent), or separated (4 percent), or had husbands whose earnings in 1981 were less than $15,000 (21 percent).[2]
Women are out ill more than men; they cost the company more.	A Public Health Service study shows little difference in the absentee rate due to illness or injury: 5.6 days a year for women, 5.2 days for men.
Women do not work as long or as regularly as their male co-workers; their training is costly—and largely wasted.	A declining number of women leave work for marriage and children. Even among those who do leave, a majority return when their children are in school.[1]

The Myth	*The Reality*
	In 1977, the average woman 16 years old could expect to spend 27.7 years of her life in the work force, compared with 38.5 years for men.[2] The single woman averaged 45 years. Studies on labor turnover indicate that net differences for men and women are generally small.[1]
Women should stick to "women's jobs" and should not compete for "men's jobs."	Job requirements, with extremely rare exceptions, are unrelated to sex. Tradition rather than job content has led to labeling certain jobs as women's and others as men's. In measuring 22 inherent aptitudes and knowledge areas, a research laboratory found that there is no sex difference in 14, women excel in 6, and men excel in 2.
Women do not want responsibility on the job; they do not want promotions or job changes that add to their load.	Relatively few women have been offered positions of responsibility. When given these opportunities, women, like men, do cope with job responsibility in addition to personal or family demands. In 1973, 4.7 million women held professional and technical jobs, another 1.6 million worked as nonfarm managers and administrators. Many others held supervisory jobs at all levels in offices and factories.

The Myth	*The Reality*
The employment of mothers leads to juvenile delinquency.	Studies show that many factors must be considered when seeking causes of juvenile delinquency; a mother's working status does not appear to be a determining factor. These studies indicate that it is the quality of a mother's care rather than the time consumed in such care that is of major significance.
Men do not like to work for women supervisors.	Most men who complain about women supervisors have never worked for a woman. In one study, in which at least ¾ of both the male and female respondents (all executives) had worked with women managers, the evaluation of women in management was favorable. On the other hand, the study showed a traditional/cultural bias among those who reacted unfavorably. In another survey, in which 41 percent of the reporting firms indicated that they hired women executives, none rated their performance as unsatisfactory, 50 percent rated them adequate, 42 percent rated them the same as their predecessors, and 8 percent rated them better than their predecessors.[1]

1. United States Department of Labor (1974).
2. United States Department of Labor (1982).

Another myth that illustrates the incongruence between a concept of leadership and images of females is the notion that women do not want to achieve high-level positions because they have an internal motive called "fear-of-success." Thus, bright women who have the potential to be successful may avoid high-level achievement due to a stable personality factor. This was closely examined in the late 1960's and early 1970's. To test the phenomenon, Horner (1972) asked subjects to write brief stories to follow the lead: "At the end of first term finals Anne/John finds herself/himself at the top of her/his medical school class." In scoring the stories, fear-of-success was judged present if any of the following were in the stories:

1. Expectations of negative consequences from success: social rejection, loss of friends, date or marriage partner ineligibility, and isolation, loneliness, or unhappiness.
2. Indications of conflict about success: doubts about femininity or normality, guilt, or despair about success.
3. Denial of effort or responsibility for attaining the success.
4. Bizarre or inappropriate responses: hostility or confusion.

A fear-of-success response to the story lead might be: Anne knows that all her friends will hate her for doing so well and decides to drop out of medical school. Given the four criteria above, the results of the study indicated that more than 65 percent of the women and less than 10 percent of the men ($p < .0005$)* demonstrated fear-of-success (Horner, 1972). The research implied that one of the reasons women were not found in prominent positions in our society was that females feared success and therefore avoided achievement.

Subsequent research, however, indicated that fear-of-success changed according to certain variables in the situation. Olsen and Willemsen (1978) altered the context of some of the story leads by including a statement that "half of her classmates are men and half are women." The percentage of fear-of-success stories by women was lower in the mixed class. Furthermore, the

*The probability of difference occurring by chance is less than .0005.

Olsen and Willemsen study indicated that women perceive more positive than negative outcomes from success and that if negative consequences occur, they are more likely to be from the reactions of other people than from an internal personality variable. Thus, underachievement by women in our society more likely results from cultural and social restrictions rather than from an internal trait in women (Olsen & Willemsen, 1978; Condry & Dyer, 1976).

The leadership literature indicates that there have been cultural assumptions and myths about women and leadership that may have hindered women in the workplace. Research has been debunking the mythology and replacing stereotypes with more accurate information about female leaders. Challenges are being raised to the perception, not only of female leaders, but to leadership behaviors in general.

3

Overt and Covert Curriculum

Because evidence indicates that many leadership behaviors are learned rather than strictly inherent, female and male educators have reexamined curricular offerings for students in various disciplines. The basic issue is how higher-education institutions prepare students to take their place in the education profession.

THE CURRICULUM

Studying to obtain a degree is one of the necessary credentials for joining the profession. During the training time, students demonstrate their ability to perform professional work, master core knowledge, and demonstrate professional skills. It is also a time when students are socialized into the profession—they learn its norms and expectations. Thus, two kinds of learning occur during the student years—the overt, formal training that is listed in the college catalog and the covert, informal training that is not listed in any catalog. The overt curriculum lists required courses, options for courses of study, minimum gradepoint, and so forth. The informal curriculum shapes the vision each student has of herself or himself in the profession (Coombs, 1978) and may be more important for women who have the potential to be leaders than the formal curriculum.

Undergraduate formal training appears to be the same for women and men. It parallels the universal criteria system used in some areas of government, in which core courses are required for all students in a professional program and a minimum grade on tests in each course may be necessary before a student passes the course. This training system does not give the impression of treating women and men differently. A closer look, however, may reveal a very different experience for women and men. There may be a "hidden curriculum," which has been defined as the "unplanned and unrecognized values taught and learned through the process of schooling. [Further, the] implicit values inferred from consistencies in teacher behavior and in class organization and procedures have been assumed to have an extensive impact on the values, norms, and behaviors of students" (Bain, 1976). The hidden curriculum may affect women differently from men. The four most common patterns of disparities in education, which contribute to informal training and which may affect leadership by women, are:

1. The omission of women from the language and content of programs or, according to Daly (1973), the "silence" about women.
2. Inaccurate information about women or misinterpretations of research data (Oglesby, 1978).
3. Different treatment for female and male students.
4. The absence of high-level female role models (Carnegie Commission, 1973).

Each of these factors can give female students erroneous beliefs about women and detract from the female student's potential vision of herself as a leader in the profession.

The absence of women from the language and content of courses is a serious omission, which may leave students with the belief that women did not contribute to the formation of the physical activity professions, and that they do not have a rich heritage. Indeed, unlike some disciplines, women have been leaders in the physical activity professions, and from them at least one college president has emerged. Further, women have chaired sex-separated departments, authored publications, and presented lectures (Spears, 1979). When the contributions of women, past and present, are included in the curriculum, the female students' interest in and future contributions to the field may be enhanced by reinforcing an image of women, as a group, actively participating for the advancement of the profession.

Inaccurate information about women may also diminish their potential contributions. One source of inaccurate information has been incomplete data on female subjects in research studies (Oglesby, 1976). Some researchers have assumed a similarity between women and men. For example, if men are subjects in a study and perform a certain way, women will perform the same. The assumption, however, is not tested by inclusion of women in the research studies. Since systematic research studies are usually used to build theories, this practice has led to theories that simply may not be accurate for both women and men.

Another source of inaccuracy has been the misinterpretation of research data (Parlee, 1978). Physiological differences or performance differences between the sexes may have been interpreted as indicative of the inherent inferiority of women in physical activities (Oglesby, 1978). For example, the lower performance scores of women on tasks like the softball throw may be attributed to differences in joint structure, weaker muscles, and a general lack of strength. However, recent data suggest that early training and cultural reinforcement could seriously confound the performance of both men and women on this task. In a study by Grimditch and Sockolov (Wilmore, 1977), when scores were recorded according to dominant and nondominant arm, no significant differences between the sexes were found on nondominant arm scores. The results suggest that training influenced the differences between the sexes for the dominant arm scores. The malleability of performance has also been found in other studies. At West Point, women cadets significantly increased their maximum oxygen consumption following a vigorous training program (Stauffer, 1977). Hudson (1978) gives evidence for the link between physical performance, training, and cultural expectations. Thus, interpretation of research data is somewhat subjective and may reflect inaccuracies that diminish the way women feel about themselves (Oglesby, 1978) and other women in sport.

Female students, in relation to male students, may receive different treatment in the classroom. This treatment may affect their image of themselves in the profession. A study with young children demonstrated that teachers tended to give more attention to boys, encourage them to problem-solve, and give them more individual instruction on how to do things (Serbin & O'Leary, 1975). One researcher-teacher reported timing her interactions with students in a tennis class. Much more time was spent observing, correcting, and talking to male students than to female students. The subtle message communicated through the time differential may have been that male students are worth more than female students (Hoferek, 1980b). Similar behaviors may be shown by post-secondary teachers and may affect potential female leaders. Another study (Hoferek, 1982) suggests that teachers' sex-stereotypic expectations may be stronger in co-ed physical education classes than in sex-separated physical education classes.

Teacher expectations are an important component of the classroom environment because the self-fulfilling prophecy phenomenon may affect student performance. Essentially, those who support this phenomenon assert that students read teachers' unspoken expectations for high or low performance and behave according to those expectations (Rosenthal & Jacobsen, 1968). Thus, teachers who expect stereotypic behaviors—low performance in motor skills and few leadership behaviors by women—are apt to communicate these expectations to female students, who (unless aware of the process) will act accordingly, reinforcing the teachers' beliefs.

Different treatment may also take the form of overt discrimination: in medicine, female students report being taunted, teased, and baited by teachers (Spiro, 1975); sex bias has been reported in lectures and medical clinic settings (Walsh, 1979). The use of sexist humor can be destructive to female professionals (Hoferek & Sarnowski, 1981).

Thus, the covert or hidden curriculum can be an important factor in the vision each student develops of herself as a professional. Women students should look for the common patterns of disparate training and should be aware of how their undergraduate training is affecting their vision of themselves. If discriminatory patterns are found, each woman must decide what she can do to reduce the impact of discrimination on herself and how a positive self-image can be fostered in the sexist environment.

Regardless of covert training, thousands of women complete their bachelor's degree in the activity professions each year, according to the National Center for Education Statistics (1984) (Table 3-1).

Table 3-1
Bachelor's Degrees Earned by Women, 1980–81

Subject	*Total Students*	*Women*	*Percent (Women)*
Physical education	19,095	9,570	50.1
Parks and recreation management	5,729	3,506	61.2

Graduate schools also have formal and informal elements in their programs but tend to be less structured than undergraduate programs. The admissions process itself is more subjective. Rather than a college or university central admissions office, a departmental committee or even one professor who is in charge of a particular area may make the decision to admit certain graduate students. In programs that attract many more applicants than can be admitted (e.g., medical schools), the subjective nature of admissions decisions has been challenged. In medicine, for example, many of the applicants who apply are probably capable of completing medical school and would make excellent physicians. The number of applicants admitted, however, is limited and decisions about who enters medical schools involve an element of subjectivity.

During graduate school, there is heavy reliance on an informal, protégé system of training. While some coursework is required, a graduate faculty member or mentor is responsible for training the graduate student in areas that usually are not covered in the coursework. Frequently, mentors for graduate students provide training in research design, data analysis, computer programming, data management, and research report writing. In addition, they may assist the graduate student in the publication process by critiquing manuscripts, writing letters to editors, discussing the work with potential reviewers, and suggesting likely publication outlets. Since the protégé system is more subjective than the universal criteria system, the difficulties undergraduate women face may be exacerbated at the graduate level.

Mentors may also be instrumental in obtaining financial assistance for their protégés. Usually fellowships, project assistantships, teaching assistantships, and research assistantships are available through a process that appears to be uniform for both sexes. In reality, who gets what kind of support may be a subjective process that has a depreciative impact on women because each type of assistance provides different experiences and the development of different skills. Teaching assistantships are beneficial if the student has never taught before or can lecture in the area he or she will be teaching after graduation. Usually, graduate students "progress" from teaching assistantships to other, more challenging types of financial aid. Research assistantships are important training programs in which graduate students learn the essentials of research and from which, if the mentor is amenable, the student may begin publishing research articles. Project assistantships can be clerical positions, which probably will not help the student, or administrative positions that may provide important experience in administering programs. A fellowship is considered a plum because the student can work free from other time commitments. Thus, a factor students may consider in selecting a mentor is his or her track record for obtaining funds for female graduate students.

A related problem is the lack of research training for women in the activity professions. An essential component of graduate work is research training. The most successful researchers have been trained in every aspect of the research endeavor by their mentors, in addition to taking formal research courses. Data from other disciplines state that women do not receive this comprehensive training as often as men do. Other major stumbling blocks to research training for women are a tendency for women to be employed as teaching assistants rather than research assistants, informal counseling away from such training, and a paucity of research mentors who take women seriously (Ekstrom, 1978). The results of this differential training are extremely serious for female professionals because publication and generation of external funds are directly tied to research skills and are vital to professional advancement in some institutions.

Another area in which the protégé system may break down for female graduate students, particularly doctoral students, is the quality and amount of interaction time with faculty members. In a study of graduate students from various disciplines, Holmstrom and Holmstrom (1974) concluded that faculty attitudes toward and availability to students seemed important determinants of student satisfaction and performance. Male students recorded a more favorable interaction rate with faculty members than female students. At least one of three female doctoral students reported increased emotional stress and decreased commitment to staying in graduate school in relation to a perception of the faculty's negative attitudes toward women. Not being taken seriously as a student and more overt negative behaviors, therefore, were linked to greater emotional stress and increased possibilities for attrition by female doctoral students.

Female graduate students are more likely to be returning students and may be older than men who are graduate students. Research in other disciplines notes the special challenges for reentering women (those who dropped out of training, usually to have a family or to teach for several years). Some of the difficulties are feelings of isolation, feelings of inadequacy, a lack of mentors, fears about "fitting in," balancing commitments, inadequate female networks (Regents' Task Force on the Status of Women, 1981), disappointment that they had "dropped out," exclusion from socialization into the profession and from other signs of belonging, and lack of recognition (White, 1970).

On the other hand, reentry women may have much to offer to graduate programs. Many continue their education because they are deeply interested in a discipline and are attracted to scholarship and scientific research. Despite their discontinuous educational pattern, these women may have a commitment to learning and excellence (White, 1970). Furthermore, women age twenty-two and over are the fastest growing college student population (Bernay, 1978) and institutions will have to become more sensitive to their needs.

Female graduate students, like their undergraduate counterparts, may be treated differently from men in the classroom. The psychological literature indicates that subtle processes, which often are unintentional, can produce discrimination:

Asking males to answer questions more often than females.

Asking females questions that require only rote memory but asking males questions that require analytic reasoning or similar higher order processes.

> Selecting females only as examples of poor work, never as positive examples.
>
> Selecting males more frequently than females to demonstrate a process or model positive behavior. (Ekstrom, 1978)

In some cases, women report being "cooled out" of classrooms and laboratory participation (Ekstrom, 1978).

Other differences in treatment have been reported by female graduate students. Women state that they "receive no encouragement for their work, meet implications that scholarship is unfeminine, meet indifference to their training, and find faculty reluctance to find them aid or jobs." Some faculty tell female students that they will not be able to get jobs in major universities and in other ways are less supportive of women than of men (Ekstrom, 1978).

Nonetheless, women have obtained graduate degrees. During 1980–81, women achieved 1,975 of the total 4,219 master's degrees (46.8 percent) and 83 of the 222 doctoral degrees (37.4 percent) in physical education; in parks and recreation management, women earned 340 of the 643 master's degrees (52.9 percent) and 12 of the 42 doctoral degrees (28.6 percent) (National Center for Education Statistics, 1984). Furthermore, during the time that statistics were compiled for the aggregated degrees in physical education, health, and recreation, women earned 783 of the 2,861 doctoral degrees (27.4 percent) from 1920–72 (Scientific Manpower Commission, 11/78). Thus, while the proportion of women steadily declines as the level of the degree increases, women have achieved and are continuing to achieve a significant proportion of the advanced degrees in the profession over a number of years.

Both undergraduate and graduate female students share some difficulties that are related to the informal curriculum. Sexual harassment has become a prevalent problem on some campuses. It includes verbal or other expressive behavior commonly considered by persons of a particular sex and of average sensibilities to be demeaning to themselves. This conduct either seriously interferes with the academic work of a student(s) or makes the instructional setting hostile or intimidating, or demeaning to students of a particular sex and of average sensibilities (University of Wisconsin Faculty Senate Minutes, 2 March 1981).

Sexist curricula, both formal and informal, may result in failure of the socialization process for those who complete degrees or attrition of talented women from physical activity programs. When a double standard and unfairness are recognized, frustration and anger may follow. A perceptive woman may feel more and more isolated as the discrimination continues, particularly if it is not countered (Hilberman et al., 1975). Unless sexism is countered or reduced, the socialization process may fail. The woman may not incorporate an image of the "ideal professional" into her sense of self and, indeed, may feel alienated from the profession.

The difficulties of the college or university situation may also cause women to drop out. Among the reasons for the high dropout rate among female doctoral students at the University of California at Berkeley were "poor advisory procedures, exclusion of women from informal communication networks, from apprentice or collegial relationships with faculty, indifference of faculty, and confusions resulting from lack of information about criteria for evaluation, and about funding, success, job possibilities, etc." (Sells, 1976). A factor that was within the control of the students, but contributed to the high dropout rate, was a feeling that the problems were personal rather than, in reality, shared by most female graduate students. Other problems stemmed from lowered self-confidence and self-esteem, ambivalence about the conflicts between career demands and personal life demands, conflicts between teaching and research interests, and alienation produced by feelings of powerlessness. There were also feelings of infantilization and demoralization caused by faculty attitudes. To counter some of the problem areas, women have joined together to form caucuses. When women's caucuses became active at Berkeley the differential in dropout rates between women and men declined to zero over the six-year period examined (Sells, 1976).

The reduction of attrition is not the only benefit to be gained when women group together. Women's colleges have provided valuable training experience for female leaders. In single-sex situations, women must, and do, lead. Furthermore, single-sex institutions are sensitive to the needs of women. White (Kaplan, undated) maintains that a women's college is "not a college without men, we are a college *for* women. We are not a protective community; we are a strengthening and reinforcing community."

Women's groups may provide the basis for valuable professional networking. Cohorts of men who graduated together have traditionally helped each other in their professional lives. For example, lawyers in the legal-profession network choose judges, governors, key chairpersons, and legislative leadership. When individual lawyers were asked why they helped a colleague, a frequent response was "he was in my class" or "he went to school when I did." The helping lawyer knows the favor will be returned if an opportunity arises. The same system of reciprocal supportive networking can help women advance to positions on sports boards, administrative search committees, high-level faculty offices, committees for rule changes, or association offices. Someone in a network can boost another woman's career and, in turn, expect to receive assistance from her colleague (Doderer, 1979).

Students experience overt and covert training during the process of becoming a professional. Recent research indicates that the covert or hidden curriculum may diminish the way female students feel about themselves and about other women in the profession. Scholarly work indicates that the socialization of women away from leadership positions may have been part of an unconscious process.

Awareness of the hidden curriculum and how it may diminish potential female leaders is the first step in breaking the covert socialization process. Clarifying the skills needed to lead and structuring situations to practice those skills, possibly through single-sex groups, is helpful. The literature also suggests that women need to establish networks to assist each other—not only into positions—but in shaping a positive image of themselves as leaders.

4

Women As Faculty and Professionals

Many women have achieved credentials from educational institutions and joined the professional ranks. However, the distribution of women, by discipline and within discipline, suggests patterns of segregation and exclusion—some disciplines and subdisciplines either have no women or are almost completely filled with women. Within disciplines and certain institutions there are no women in the highest positions of the status hierarchies. Given the patterns, one could question where the potential female leaders have gone, why they are not in positions of power, and what can be done.

Status In The Profession

Since the early 1970's, concern has been voiced about the collective "place" of women in education. In particular, the Carnegie Commission conducted one of the most comprehensive studies on women in the education profession. Based on the data collected, the Carnegie Commission report (1973) concluded (Figure 4-1):

1. Women are underutilized in education, that is, if you compare expected and actual employment patterns, there are—with some exceptions—fewer women than expected.
2. The higher the position, the greater the underutilization of women, that is, the pyramiding pattern found for the careers of men is similar for women except the proportions of women in the upper levels is markedly smaller than expected.
3. Situational or external variables in educational institutions, rather than variables within the women themselves, produced a "systems effect" or "ecosystem" which, if

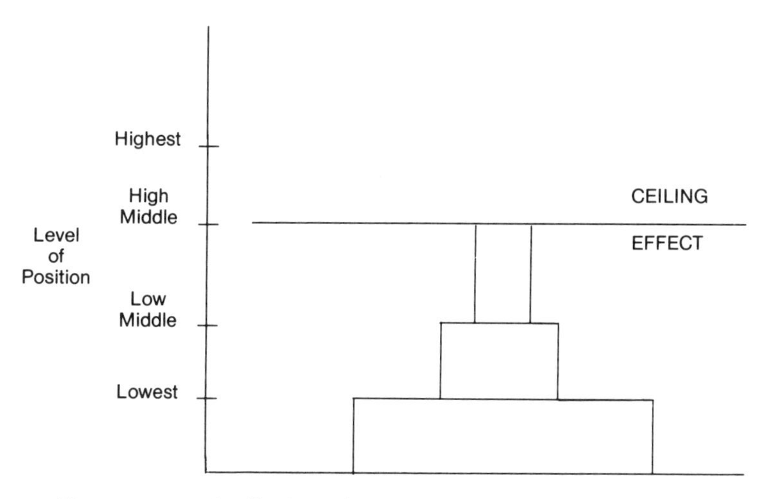

Figure 4-1. Distribution of women in educational institutions. Ceiling Effect is a point on the career ladder beyond which, inexplicably, almost no women are found.

unchanged, would perpetuate the underutilization of women in education.

While these data may be true for education in general, one could certainly question the validity for physical education. After all, physical education has a heritage of sex-separated departments through which women have advanced into leadership positions. There are suggestions, however, that the patterns in the Carnegie Commission report are true for the physical education profession as well as for general education. Data collected in 1977 (Hoferek, 1980a) reveal that differences exist between women and men on traditional indicators of career status, such as degrees earned ($X^2 = 43.26$, df $= 2$, $p < .001$), institutional position ($X^2 = 13.43$, df $= 2$, $p < .001$), and salary ($X^2 = 30.18$, df $= 3$, $p < .0001$).* The data indicate that the percentages of women and men earning advanced degrees differ markedly (Figure 4-2), with a higher percentage of men earning

*X^2 (chi square), statistical test of significance; df, the degree of freedom; $p < .001$ or .0001, probability that the differences occurred by chance is less than 1/1000 or 1/10,000, or the test showed that the differences were statistically significant.

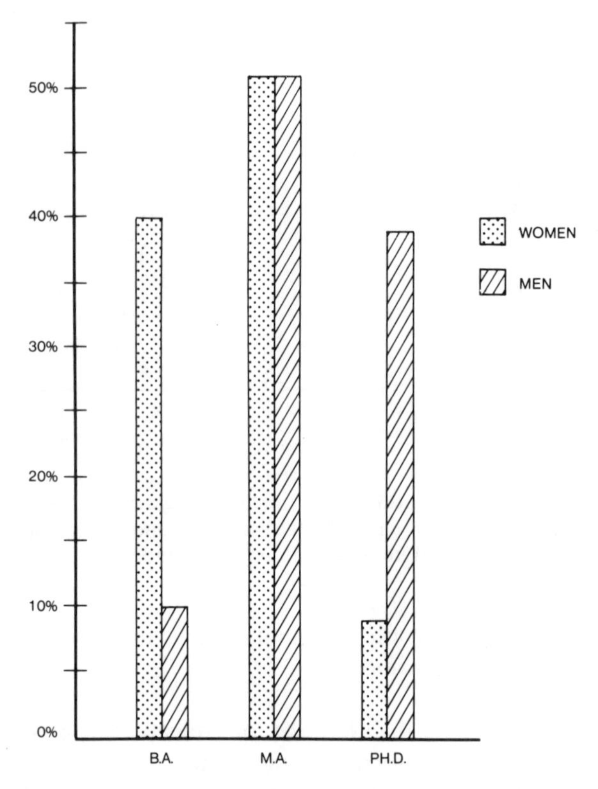

Figure 4-2. Degrees for men and women in physical education.

doctorates. Similarly, a higher percentage of men are employed in colleges and universities (Figure 4-3) and earn over $20,000 (Figure 4-4). In regard to salaries, it should be noted that when years of teaching experience, degrees earned, institutional position, and whether or not a person coached are controlled, significant differences still exist between women and men, with men earning the higher salaries.

Earlier studies are consistent with the Hoferek (1980a) data. Although 40 percent of both the men and the women wanted to be teacher-researchers, women were hired more often as activity teachers (Table 4-1) and spent more of their working time on duties relating to teaching (Table 4-2). Women taught lower-

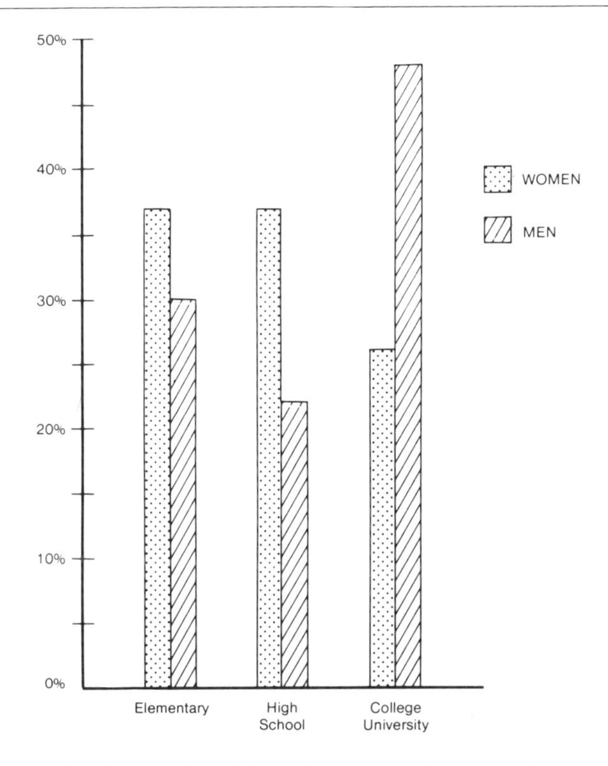

Figure 4-3. Institutional positions for men and women in physical education.

level classes more frequently (Table 4-3), although both sexes wanted teaching assignments in the higher levels (Fallon, 1973).

Based on the data, Fallon concluded that female doctorates were shortchanged in the marketplace. They received lower positions than the men and lower positions than their level of aspiration would warrant. Confined to the lower levels of teaching, these women bore heavier loads and, therefore, their opportunities for research and publication were limited. To deal with these problems, the following recommendations were made: encourage women to complete the doctorate in less time, encourage women to be represented in all areas, promote equal opportunity in employment, and encourage new courses to meet the needs of women (Fallon, 1973).

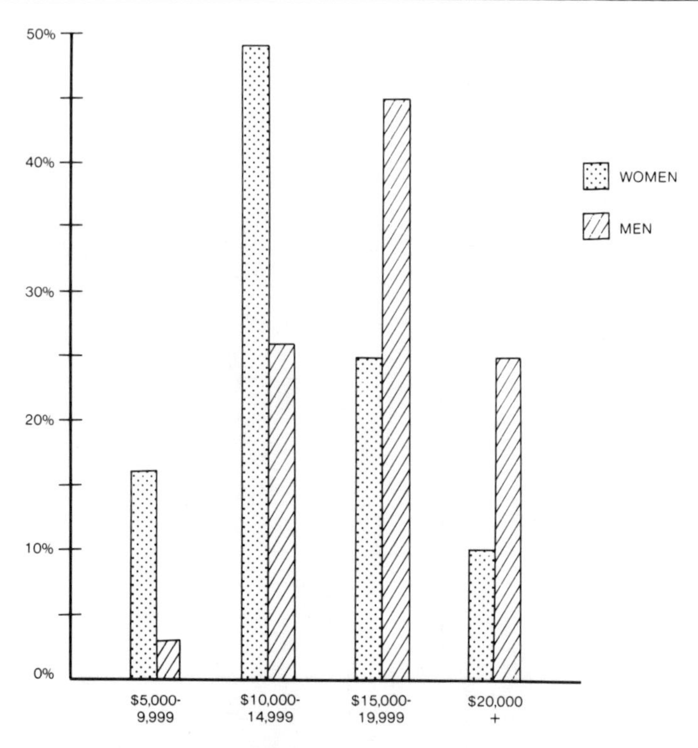

Figure 4-4. Salaries for men and women in physical education. (By Dori Gordon, Rockford School of Medicine.)

Table 4-1
Initial Position of New PhDs

Employment	*Percentages* Women	Men
Primarily activity teachers	40	13
Theory teachers	40	35
Administrators or teacher-researchers	20	21 administer 18 teach-research 8 coach 5 research

Table 4-2
Working Duties of New PhDs

Teaching Time Duties	*Percentages* Women	*Men*
Teaching duties	75	53
Administration	20	25
Research	5	12
Coaching	5	10

Table 4-3
Level of Assignment for New PhDs

Student Assignment	*Percentages* Women	*Men*
Freshman and sophomore	56	40
Junior and senior	36	48
Graduate	8	12

Surveys of the profession give additional information on women in the physical activity field and about the field in relation to others in higher education. A comparison of American Association of University Professors (AAUP) and physical education salary data indicates that salaries for the profession fall below the fortieth percentile for institutions offering the doctorate and, with the exception of full professors, below the midpoint in institutions granting bachelor's degrees. There is also a definite salary difference between faculty who teach only undergraduate and those who teach graduate students. Administrators receive the highest salaries, teachers the lowest (Belanger & Everett, 1973). Over 1,200 physical educators participated in a study by Ashcraft (1973) that controlled type of institutions, rank, degree, and sex. Tests between groups yielded twenty-one significant "t" tests,* and every significant result showed that men earned higher salaries. The same study indicated that the professionals who worked in buildings constructed prior to 1920 were

*A "t" test is a statistical tool used to determine if there is a significant difference between two means (Miller, 1970).

generally women. Women also held proportionately less than their share of the top ranks. The men in this study were promoted faster than the women. Other results indicated that men taught more graduate courses, women were involved in more skill classes than their rank would predict, men taught fewer credit hours and had fewer class-contact hours per week, men had less committee work, and, when rank and degree were equalized, the men had higher salaries.

In view of the statistics, it is ironic that most physical educators feel that men and women have comparable degrees, ranks, salaries, facilities, philosophies, influence, representation, teaching loads, and an equal share of the budget (Davies, 1973). One hundred thirty-eight men and 120 women voiced those feelings in the Davies survey. These subjective views are highly discrepant with more objective data.

One approach, therefore, to examining leadership in a particular discipline is to compare the numbers of women and men, using various indicators of leadership, such as highest degree earned, institutional position, and salary. With these criteria, the patterns identified by the Carnegie Commission—that women appear to be underutilized and the higher the position, the greater the underrepresentation of women—are to be found in the physical education profession.

Another approach to examining leadership is to look at the power of a particular group in a profession. For example, a group may be a numerical minority, but hold powerful positions from which it exerts leadership. This area is much more difficult to measure, but the little evidence gathered recently indicates that women have even less power and leadership than expected:

1. Women who achieve the doctorate in physical education are frequently placed in initial positions unbefitting their preparation and aspiration (Fallon, 1973).
2. Only a small percentage of women publish research articles or are members of AAHPERD's Research Consortium for experienced researchers (Safrit, 1979).
3. Women are losing representation in power positions, such

as head of department or chair of graduate program (Fox, 1977).

Therefore, the statistical patterns and the more subjective indicators coincide and demonstrate that physical education has the same problems as some other disciplines—the underutilization of women who could be leaders and the underrepresentation of women at the highest levels in the profession.

Similar patterns are found in athletic positions. While there was a 37 percent increase in the number of coaches for women during the 1974–79 time span, there was a significant decrease in female head coaches and a concomitant increase in the number of male head coaches (Holmen & Parkhouse, 1981). The trend was summarized in data collected by King (1984) (Table 4-4). Furthermore, the percentage of female athletic directors is declining. The proportion of female athletic directors for women's sports declined from 61 percent in 1976 to 55 percent in 1978 (Burke, 1979). There have also been declining opportunities for female officials. In the past, most women's events were officiated by women who were certified by the National Association for Girls and Women in Sports (NAGWS). Recently, men have increasingly become eligible and have been hired by the male athletic directors (Geadelmann et al., 1985).

Status In Coeducational Institutions

One of the greatest challenges to the representation of women in leadership positions is the move from sex-separated to sex-integrated departments. In physical education, many sex-separated departments changed to co-ed units during the 1960's and 1970's. In athletics, the National Collegiate Athletic Association

Table 4-4
Coaches for Women's Intercollegiate Teams

Coaches	*Percentages* 1970–71	1975–76	1980–81
Male	8.6	24.7	41.6
Female	91.4	75.3	58.4

(NCAA), the historical governing body for men's athletics, struggled with the Association for Intercollegiate Athletics for Women (AIAW) for control of the growing programs for college and university women. After a lengthy contest, which included taking its case to an appeals court, the AIAW lost—the traditional men's governing body gained control of the programs for women (Fields, 1984).

The combining of sex-separated educational units is not without precedent in the education profession. In medicine, women's medical colleges operated for approximately fifty years. "When the women's colleges closed or merged with male institutions, the total number of female faculty positions in medical schools was sharply curtailed" (Walsh, 1979). For example, the New York Infirmary Medical College merged with Cornell University Medical School. Thirteen years later, "Cornell did not have a single woman on the teaching staff or in its clinical service. [Emily Blackwell], who had enthusiastically endorsed the New York Infirmary's absorption by Cornell in 1899, admitted that 'it cut short the teaching careers of a group of capable and rising young women teachers' " (Walsh, 1979). The merger meant the loss of institutions that "seem to have stimulated research and clinical practices which improved the delivery and health care to women patients (Walsh, 1979). In addition, female physicians provided liaison to women's rights organizations and, in turn, were supported by feminists. Post-doctoral opportunities were offered by female-operated hospitals. Thus, before the mergers with men's programs, women's medical colleges provided opportunities for women-centered research, skill development, and a supportive environment.

The data from other single-sex colleges that have gone co-ed is also disheartening; the position of women diminishes. When Vassar became co-ed, "the percentage of full-time female faculty dropped from 42.9 percent in 1967–68, a year before coeducation, to 38.2 percent in 1973–74. The percentage of female department chairpersons dropped from 38 percent to 19 percent in this period. However, the percentage of female instructors, lecturers, and nonladder appointments increased from 50 percent in 1967–68 to 70 percent in 1973–74," according to Baker (Kaplan, n.d.).

In physical education, the merging of men's and women's departments raised concern about the potential loss of female leaders (Hoferek, 1980a). As departments became co-ed, women lost "a disproportionate number of top positions" to men (Rulings, 1976). For example, an examination of the Big Ten universities indicated that nine physical-education units (divisions, schools, departments) are combined. In those nine, seven top administrators are men, one is a woman, and one could not be determined because no first name was given (*Gold Book*, 1982).

In addition to administrative losses, traditionally single-sex organizations, such as The National Association of Physical Education for College Women, have been disbanded in favor of co-ed organizations. "Like single-sex women's colleges, women's groups in physical education provided unique opportunities for females to experience and learn leadership skills. In the single-sex groups women chaired organizations and committees, presented papers, looked to other females and themselves for leadership, obtained visibility, had role models, [and] could find a forum for their concerns" (Hoferek, 1980a). Without the single-sex organizations to provide leadership training, alternative development strategies will have to be used (Hoferek, 1980a).

Status As Mentors And Protégés

The successful outcome of women's struggle in sex-integrated departments is critical for future generations of female professionals. It cannot be emphasized enough that role models are important determinants of how neophyte professionals see themselves and that, by serving as mentors, successful women may be gate openers and in other ways facilitate women's careers. The influence of women who chaired departments was recorded by Ashcraft (1973). When women chaired departments, other women generally had better employment conditions: a higher proportion held professional rank, had lighter credit-hour loads, had the opportunity to teach summer school, and were satisfied with their rate of promotion and with their salaries.

Women who are already established may actively assist

upcoming professionals by serving as mentors. The mentor concept has been considered so important by some college and university departments that a mentor is assigned to new members until they are tenured. The mentor relationship tends to be gratifying for professors. They express great satisfaction when their students do well and they feel that they had a role in these achievements (Mokros, Erkut, & Spichiger, 1981). On the graduate level especially, there may be direct benefits for mentors. According to Kammer (Oglesby, 1981), a feedback system between mentors and protégés is established. For example, successful students are more likely to co-author papers with their mentor and to cite the mentor's work, and increased visibility will enhance the mentor's status.

However, perceptions of mentor patterns differ for female and male mentors. In a college-level study, most female and male professors saw themselves in the role of teacher or advisor; only a few described themselves as mentors. Female mentors were more likely to talk in terms of friendship with their protégés; the men emphasized their role as colleague, mentor, or adviser. Male professors were more likely to feel that they initiated the relationship or that the relationship was mutually decided upon. No female professors felt that they initiated the mentoring process, although a few said that the relationship was mutually decided upon. Most women felt that the students initiated the process (Mokros, Erkut, & Spichiger, 1981). If the professors' perceptions are accurate, students who want female mentors will probably have to initiate the relationship.

Most mentors felt that they influenced their students' academic work by opening up new areas, giving a solid background in a discipline, and encouraging new interests. Some mentors, particularly women, were uncomfortable with the idea of influencing students, saying that they made a conscious decision to avoid too much influence (Mokros, Erkut, & Spichiger, 1981). Female mentors were more likely to note the personal aspects of the relationship. This was particularly true for women with female protégés; the female professors in this category felt that they were role models for aspiring young women. Men who mentored men, however, said almost nothing about personal influence (Mokros, Erkut, & Spichiger, 1981).

In the workplace, the protégé system commonly operates in the higher levels of most professions and may be part of the continuing socialization process that occurs during the first decade of professional life. Mentors may actively promote their protégés' work by influencing who reads the articles or papers, who listens to the reports, and who provides friendly reviews and suggestions for drafts of papers. In addition, there are avenues of advancement that can only be known by people who are insiders, for example, who has grant money for specific projects (White, 1970). A mentor can facilitate the entrance of neophytes into the inner circles of a profession, where shared norms and attitudes, a high degree of informality, and a tendency toward homogeneity hinder unmentored individuals (Epstein, 1970).

For certain high-level positions, a person has to be "in" to learn the job. Trade secrets and the latest professional innovations are shared informally well before they are disseminated formally (Epstein, 1970)—the latest techniques, research discoveries, and publications may be given to colleagues years before they are published in professional journals. Since some journals are backlogged for several years, the informal system serves to update the circle of professionals who are sharing their work.

This informal process may be a disadvantage for female professionals. The mentor is more likely to be male than female and may have mixed feelings about having a female protégé. It is not as easy for a male sponsor to identify with a woman and to see her as his likely successor. Furthermore, the sponsor's wife may resent the female protégé, who in turn may find the men in her life (i.e., husband or father) jealous or suspicious of the relationship. The female professional may also be hampered by the male mentor's belief that women are less committed to their career and are, therefore, not worth the effort (Epstein, 1970).

Some male mentors, however, may make extra efforts to enhance the career of their female protégés. The male sponsor may be aware of the difficulties women face in the professions and therefore commit himself to their assistance. The protégé relationship may be more important for female professionals than their male counterparts. Support in entering the inner circles, which male neophytes expect as a matter of course, may or may not occur under the mentor system. However, for women who have mentors this support will be more likely (Epstein, 1970).

There is evidence that some successful women have had several mentors. The mentor concept has been broadened to recognize the contributions that several individuals could make to help the neophyte professional in a career. One mentor may know a number of people in the profession and use these contacts to find job openings or advancement opportunities. Another mentor may assist with the latest research techniques. Still another may help with publications.

While not condoning it, female mentors may share with other women the unique experience of being a "stranger" in the academic milieu. Many professional women feel as if they are "outside" the profession. The stranger/outsider feeling is a common experience for which female mentors can prepare their protégés. Acknowledgment and understanding, without legitimation, can assist female protégés in overcoming the phenomenon (Oglesby, 1981). Mentors can also assist by developing and sharing coping strategies for the stranger/outsider feeling.

Although mentors for women professionals are important, the clublike atmosphere of the professions may continue to diminish the potential contributions of females. Discrimination may take the form of omissions rather than overt actions.

A general study of women with doctorates indicates a high level of productivity and commitment. Fully employed females with their doctorates published as much as their male counterparts, engaged in research, were active in professional organizations, were offered consultant positions, were more likely to be awarded fellowships, and were accepted in honorary societies. Despite their accomplishments, the women doctorates often felt left out; they felt that informal recognition and signs of belonging were lacking. In daily professional life, the women had problems finding someone to have lunch or coffee breaks with, to share an idea, or to be a research partner. Thus, the lack of informal interaction may exclude women from new ideas and lead to their feeling like strangers (White, 1970).

Women may exacerbate the exclusion problem by a reluctance

to put themselves forward or to protest their exclusion. "It is a vicious circle: men indifferent or unaware of excluding women; women insecure and hesitant of intruding" (White, 1970). Rather than solving the problem on an individual basis, however, institutions could provide overall remedies by establishing programs to bring women into the "club."

Women on some campuses have attempted to address the "club" issue positively. Luncheons, socials, and receptions for new women are an opportunity to form supportive networks. Women who are established may invite neophytes to lunch or introduce them to potential colleagues. Women's caucuses may meet regularly to discuss topics of interest to women or invite outside speakers to share their work. Researchers in similar areas may sponsor a lecture series or convene periodically to get feedback on their work. In essence, some women professionals are forming their own "club."

While the activity professions have a heritage that notes the contributions of female leaders, recent data indicate that women are not in high-level positions in the proportions one would expect. Furthermore, the position of women in the activity professions appears to be declining rather than improving. One contributing factor to the situation may be the recent merger of previously sex-separated units.

If women are to become leaders in the activity professions, they will have to find ways to overcome the gates and hurdles placed in the path of their professional development. Mentors can assist in this process, but awareness of the obstacles is important.

5

Overcoming Gates and Hurdles

It is painful to acknowledge that barriers based on discrimination by sex still exist. This may be a hard chapter to read (it was to research and write) because discrimination hurts. Unless confronted, however, unequal opportunity in education will diminish women by eroding their vision of themselves.

Therefore, even if painful, the critical step to overcome gates and hurdles in the way of professional advancement is awareness of these barriers. Barriers may be internal or external. Internal barriers may take the form of self-devaluation and, perhaps, devaluing the work of other women—unfortunately, women may actually be detrimental to the career advancement of other women. However, most discrimination is structural, or built into the system: The structure of institutions and the gatekeepers within institutions may inhibit female leadership by establishing external barriers.

By becoming aware of obstacles within institutions, women may accurately assess the situation and avoid the frequent tendency to blame themselves for not achieving their goals. An accurate perception of barriers may help women to develop strategies that will overcome the obstacles.

Minority Group Self-Hatred

A significant hurdle to overcome is the tendency of women to experience a phenomenon called minority group self-hatred. In self-hatred, a minority individual sees his or her own group through the eyes of the dominant group. Mentally, the minority person identifies with the "practices, outlook and prejudices of the dominant group" (Allport, 1958). A profound shame may be felt by the minority person about the characteristics of her or his group—for example, an immigrant may be ashamed of speaking with an accent. Since the minority person cannot completely escape his or her own group, however, he or she hates a part of himself or herself, and further, may hate himself or herself for feeling this way. Caught in a vicious circle, the minority person's self-esteem and security may be diminished by the conflict (Allport, 1958).

Shame, lack of self-confidence, and identification with the dominant group are not the only manifestations of minority group self-hatred. Minorities may actually undermine or otherwise behave aggressively toward their own group. Thus, in-group bickering and fighting may be related to minority group self-hatred (Allport, 1958).

Minority group self-hatred can work to keep low-level women down or to demote high-level women. High-level women who actively keep other women down have been called "Queen Bees" in the popular literature because, in a beehive, there is only one queen bee—any challengers are killed. Self-hatred may also cause women to undermine high-level women. Thus, as Lewis states (Hacker, 1969), behaviors associated with minority group self-hatred may take many forms: denigration of other women, acceptance of the dominant group's stereotype of women, excluding oneself from the norm of the group, scorning oneself.

Some references to minority group self-hatred are made in the physical education literature. Alexander (1973) notes that women resent other women who are successful, and indicates that the "different" women are a threat. Felshin (1974) states that women athletes who do not conform to the "feminine image" may be sacrificed or isolated despite their ability. Thus, women may disparage other women in the activity professions because of the image they elicit or because they are successful.

Trashing, which is related to minority group self-hatred, is another hurdle. Two categories of women are usually subjected to trashing: achievers and supporters. Achievers are denigrated for several reasons, including standing out in a crowd. Rather than being applauded for their excellence, the achievers may be isolated or hostilely rejected. Women who are supporters may find increasingly greater demands for their assistance until the demands become unrealistic. Ultimately, the demands cannot be met and the supporter either retreats or is trashed (Joreen, 1976).

"Sisterhood is powerful: it kills sisters." The viciousness of the trashing process is very destructive to the women involved because of its personal nature. Disagreement, conflict, or opposition are normal within any group, but trashing goes beyond these phenomena. It has been called character assassination and psychological rape. "What is attacked is not one's actions, or one's ideas, but one's self" (Joreen, 1976).

While the individuals involved experience personal pain, trashing is also a form of social control. It perpetuates distrust among women and detracts from the women who could assume leadership roles (Joreen, 1976). By keeping women apart, trashing can block the collective power of women from being recognized and used.

A related phenomenon is the role of "token." Tokens are frequently found when an institution is put under pressure to share its privileges and power with a group that has previously been excluded. The token is a member of the underrepresented group who is allowed to operate in the institution; she is usually highly visible. While the token is qualified and has credentials for her position, she is an outsider. Two frequent strictures placed on tokens are serving as gatekeepers for their own group (restricting the numerical flow of outsiders into the profession) and retaining the system they have entered (Laws, 1975).

In discussing tokens, Daly (1973) states:

> Often it happens that the woman who has achieved outstanding success . . . openly discourages other women from following her example. Having accepted her role as token in the higher echelons of the professional establishment, she adopts the attitudes of her male colleagues toward women who would aspire to follow the same road. Her words of discouragement and her lack of supportive sisterhood confuse and present a kind of "double bind" situation to women who look to her for encouragement.

In response to the damage done by women tokens to other women, Daly further asserts: "Ultimately, only women can eradicate the psychological violence done by and through women to members of our own sex, by giving support and making each other conscious of what is in large measure an unconscious process."

Among academic women who are already in leadership positions and who identify with feminism, there may be an emotional distancing that has led to the phrase, the "frigid sisterhood." It reflects a determination not to be personally involved, to deny emotion and intuition. The frigid-sisterhood members may even be conducting research on women's issues, but they studiously avoid emotion in their work and interactions. The message of their actions is clear: "To succeed, separate yourself from other women. . . . Act like a man but fight sexism" (Crawford, 1978). The frigid sisterhood confuses women who look to established women for support and encouragement.

While there are standards for entrance, retention, and advancement in the education profession, there is increasing evidence that there are also double standards—the same work and/or behavior may be evaluated differently for men and for women—that may negatively affect women who strive for leadership positions.

An early study by Goldberg (1968) required female college students to evaluate professional journal articles. The only difference in the articles was the author's name, for example, either John T. McKay or Joan T. McKay. A clear bias by women against women was indicated. Furthermore, the tendency occurred in traditionally male fields and in traditionally female fields. The researcher concluded that "there is a tendency among women to downgrade the work of professionals of their own sex."

Other researchers followed Goldberg's line of study, addressing the question of whether men also were prejudiced against women and what variables elicited the prejudiced responses. Inconsistent results were found (Peck, 1978).

A study with serious implications for women concerned about female leadership was conducted by Peck (1978). Articles with either male or female authors were evaluated by male and female subjects. The authors were ascribed high or low professional status. Biographical information for high-status authors stated that they were associate professors at a large university and had a long list of publications and honors. Low-status authors were described as doctoral candidates in education and the paper was listed as a term project. Both "male and female subjects evaluated the high-status woman significantly more favorably than the low-status woman and evaluated the low-status man significantly more favorably than the low-status woman." Furthermore, female raters were more affected by the status condition than male raters; that is, the female respondents tended to overvalue the high-status woman and to devalue the low-status woman. Based on the study, Peck concluded that the low-status woman may "receive little support from other women when she most needs it—in her initial attempts to achieve and succeed."

Since authorship is critical for professional advancement in some positions, the tendency to evaluate negatively the writing of women more than men suggests that anonymous reviews may be helpful in dealing with this area of possible discrimination. Before the adoption of an anonymous submission policy for scholarly paper presentation by the Archaeological Institute of America, 6.3 percent of the papers selected were written by female scholars. The year after the anonymous submission policy became effective, 17 percent of the papers selected were written by women (Doe, 1978).

Teaching ability may also be subject to prejudiced attitudes, according to recent research. Male and female students tended to rate female faculty lower than male faculty on teaching evaluation forms. While there was no relationship between perception of difficulty and perception of teaching effectiveness for male faculty, there was a definite relationship between those factors for female faculty. Thus, "women who were perceived as difficult graders received lower teacher evaluations relative to other women while those who were perceived as easy graders received higher teaching evaluations." The implications of these data are that different processes operate for the evaluation of male and female faculty. Female faculty may be penalized more than male faculty for having high academic standards (Unger, unpublished).

Sex bias in the evaluation of coaches is also evident. Parkhouse and Williams (unpublished) asked 80 male and 80 female high-school basketball athletes to rate hypothetical coaches. The coaches were judged on a written coaching philosophy statement and high (18-2 or 17-3) or low (3-17 or 2-18) status, which represented their season record for wins and losses. Both female and male athletes rated the male coach higher than the female coach. Male students scored the female coach even lower than the female students did. Thus, when the possible judgment variables were held constant and gender was the determining factor, female coaches were rated lower than male coaches by student athletes.

Despite the mounting evidence that women in education experience discrimination, some women continue to believe that there is no prejudice against them or other women. The "no problem" people are one of the most difficult barriers impeding the implementation of sex fairness. It is particularly difficult when the "no problem" person is in a powerful position (Vetter, Burkhardt, & Sechler, 1978).

To counter the lack of awareness about how discrimination is perpetuated, accurate information must be obtained. Training materials for educators and administrators are available to assist in the updating process (Vetter, Burkhardt, & Sechler, 1978).

Internal Devaluation

Besides the devaluation of women by others, there may also be devaluation by women within themselves. One aspect of internal devaluation may take the form of negative "scripts." Everyone "talks" to themself. The scripts tend to follow patterns, which may be positive or negative, leadership enhancing or leadership diminishing. "You made an error, stupid. How dumb can you be?" illustrates a negative script. Once called to awareness, however, negative scripts can be changed by replacing them with positive, self-supporting messages (Butler, 1976), for example, "Come on. You can do it."

Another form of internal devaluation is the "imposter phenomenon," which has emerged in therapeutic settings (Clance & Imes, 1978). During psychotherapy, women manifesting this symptom indicate that, despite their outstanding accomplishments in academic and professional work, they really are not intellectually able and have fooled other people into believing they are bright. That is, they experience a sense of intellectual phoniness and feel like imposters. Group therapy is a frequently effective alleviation for the phenomenon because the women realize that other women share the same feeling and can test the reality of their perceptions (Clane & Imes, 1978).

Racial Minority Women

Racial minority women experience many of the same barriers white women do. Other hurdles, however, are unique. "Double jeopardy" refers to the burden of both racism and sexism on racial minority women. Both "isms" interact to affect the women negatively (Myers, unpublished; Richey, 1981).

Some of the other barriers for racial minority women are invisibility, cultural and professional isolation, class oppression, biased counseling, and a lack of role models. Thus, minority women do not have a "clearly defined, institutionalized model for professional success within the dominant culture" (Richey, 1981).

External Barriers

While some gates and hurdles are within women themselves, many external factors interact to affect potential women leaders. Educational institutions are structurally complex and form "systems" (Hoferek, unpublished)—groups of interacting, interrelated, interdependent elements that form collective entities (Morris, 1976). Within the systems, many elements affect hiring, advancement decisions, and the "climate" for women.

Each educational institution has avenues or paths to leadership positions built into the system. These avenues may be formal or informal paths and there may be overt or covert criteria leading to advancement. Along the paths are individuals called "gatekeepers" (Figure 5-1): " . . . those individuals who have the options of opening the door for you, or allowing you to open it yourself, or standing in the door to block the view to the inside" (Doderer, 1979). The individuals who serve as gatekeepers develop criteria or practices that may block certain persons from getting into the institution or advancing within it (Hoferek, unpublished).

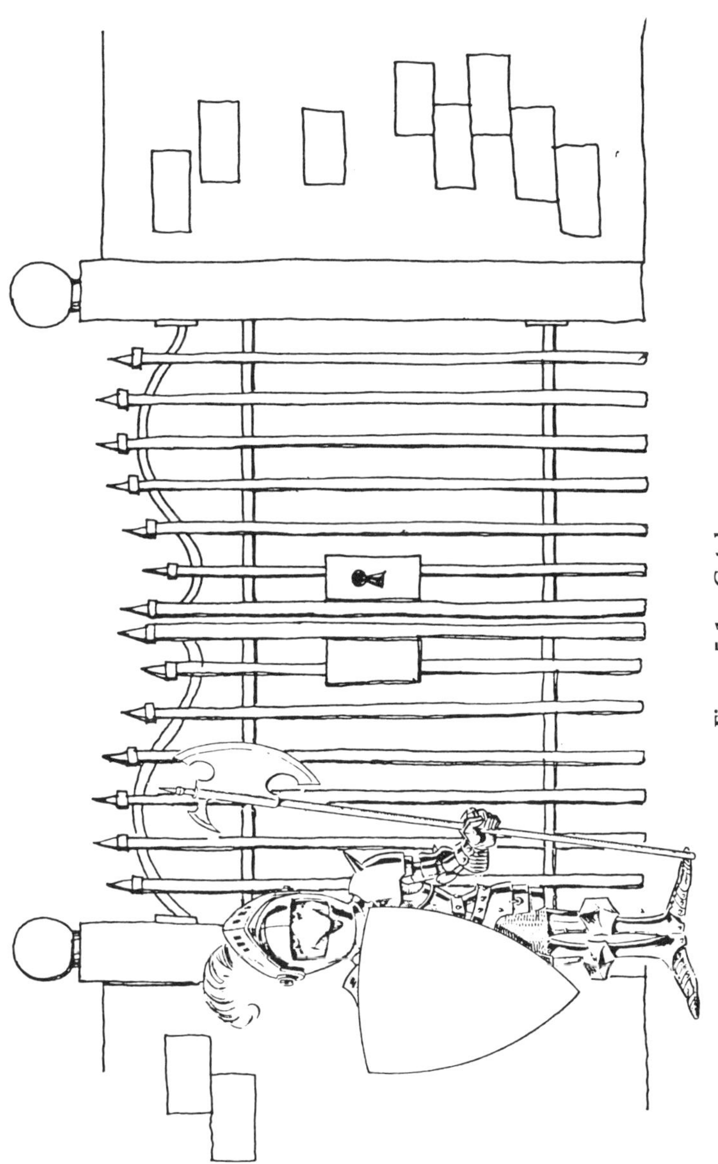

Figure 5-1. Gatekeeper.

Gatekeepers may not be consciously aware of how their actions affect various groups of people. For example, there is evidence that hiring decisions are subjective, sometimes based on whether or not the employer is comfortable with the person (Working Women, 1981) or on similarity to the person making the decision. Timpano (Bowers & Hummel, 1979) has listed other restrictive actions, which include passing on knowledge of vacancies by word-of-mouth through the buddy system, using placement services known to recommend only men, using search groups with a history of selecting only men, announcing a "possible position" and then withdrawing it if qualified women apply, limiting announcement circulation to male-intensive areas, using sexist language to convey the image of a male candidate, circulating the public advertisement close to the deadline, advertising in journals known for their circulation among men, using blind box numbers so that follow-up on who was selected is not possible, and advertising only after a candidate is already on the new job. Thus, certain groups of people can be filtered out through recruitment and selection practices.

The visibility of the hiring process influences the decisions gatekeepers make. One research study compared hypothetical hiring decisions, based on résumés from two racially different applicants, made when the decision-makers knew they would be observed and when they did not know. In the self-report or observed group, employers were more likely to treat the applicants equally. When the employers did not know they were being observed, more decisions were made on the basis of race—either favoring or disfavoring the minority person (Newman & Krzystofiak, 1979).

Visibility through enforcement of equal opportunity laws affects hiring decisions and promotion rates. For example, the Office for Federal Contract Compliance examined several banks: before enforcement, the percentage of women managers rose from 11.6 percent in 1950 to 12.2 percent in 1960; after enforcement, the percentage rose from 17.6 percent in 1970 to 31.6 percent in 1979 (Working Women, 1981).

For students, gatekeepers may be found along the paths of admission, financial aid, training during the schools years, internships (Illinois State Board of Education, 1980), and other important facets of academic life.

Awareness is the first step in overcoming the gate-and-hurdle barriers to leadership by women. Obstacles may be found within women and within institutions. After identifying the barriers, educators can structure systemic environments that are supportive of female leaders and can reap the benefits of their talents.

6

Environments Fostering Success*

More can be done to foster and enhance female leadership by structuring environments that will maximize potential. Since educational institutions are systems, many external factors impact on individuals and affect the development of leadership potential. Women may have been negatively affected in the past, but institutions can be restructured to foster a more positive environment.

Many variables interact to create an institutional environment. Those that may have the most effect on leadership by women are top management, institutional philosophy, institutional policy and implementation, a system-wide approach, internalization of equal opportunity, resources available, a front-loading system, and a system of problem identification and accountability (Figure 6-1). Signs that an institution is open to women are shown in each of the variables. (The open-system approach applies to all groups that have previously been excluded from leadership in educational institutions, but will be discussed here in relation to women [Hoferek, unpublished].) Concern with an open system may be twofold: women may want to identify organizations through which they can advance, and women may want to change institutions so that they are more accessible to themselves and other females.

One of the crucial elements for an open institution is an administration (Morino, 1980) that is aware of the issues for female leaders and is committed to advancing women in the organization. When top managers demonstrate support for leadership by women, middle managers and other employees are more likely to feel it is important.

*Much of this chapter is based on the author's experiences. Additional resources are attributed.

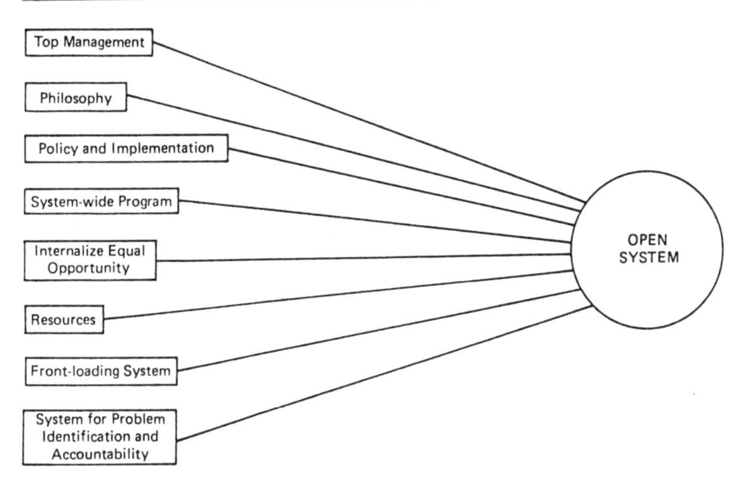

Figure 6-1. Open system.

An open system is more likely to occur when it is consistent with the organizational philosophy. If an institution bases its philosophy on equal opportunity regardless of sex, it is more likely to develop policies to reinforce that philosophy and, in turn, mechanisms to implement the policies (Hoferek, unpublished).

The open system can be identified by pervasive efforts rather than "pockets" of openness to include women. For example, there may be university-wide attempts to have women on influential committees rather than one or two departments seeking female representation. A systemwide approach is more likely to lead to the internalization or "building in" of equal opportunity. Some evidence of internalization includes variables, such as evaluations of line supervisors on performance, hiring and promotion progress for women, disciplining people who violate policies protecting women, and efforts to notify women about advancement opportunities (Hoferek, unpublished).

Open systems are characterized by an allocation of resources for equal opportunity (AAAA, 1981). Resources may be allocated for staff development for leadership training for women or awareness-raising training for colleagues. Allocation of resources may be part of the front-loading system of an institution in which funds or other rewards are not allocated until a unit is evaluated for its progress in equal opportunity. For example, a department that has not shown progress may be denied sabbatical leave money for its senior members.

Another of the crucial elements in an open system is a method for problem identification and accountability. Grievance procedures that really work to correct errors are needed to ensure fair treatment of women. Institutions are being held accountable by women's groups, such as the faculty committee in Minnesota that is monitoring the Rajender consent decree (Smetanka & Foley, 1982). Other groups, such as taxpayers, have a vested interest in seeing that educational institutions are open and use their tax support in a fair, cost-efficient manner.

While women themselves can create and improvise situations, responsible institutions "build in" certain structures that enhance the leadership potential of women. For example, the provision of daycare for the children of students, staff, and faculty alleviates some of the external role conflict women may feel. Although women may work out cooperative child-care or exchange programs, institution sponsored centers provide reliable service and, in addition, signal to the community that parenting students and employees are welcome.

Students may find support in several institutional structures: school-library resource areas with journals, newspaper-clipping files, and government documents; women's centers responsible for programs, counseling, and networking; women's studies programs, which are the academic units that focus specifically on women and are working to bring women's scholarship into the mainstream so that the historical "silence" in education is broken. All-women support groups have been established to help their members cope with educational institutions.

Reentry female students frequently wonder about their ability to complete a program. Some higher-education institutions have made adjustments for reentry women. Life experience is awarded credit in some colleges and universities so that returning students may enter with a year or two of credit. Some schools have supplemental programs to sharpen basic skills in reading and writing. Other schools may have support groups, special socials, and sororities or fraternities specifically for older students.

Women employees may find structural support for their employment. Some institutions have job sharing, in which a wife-husband team or two unrelated persons hold one job. The job sharers get full benefit coverage in medical insurance, retirement, and vacation, but are free to arrange their schedule with the other person. Parents may find that this arrangement frees them to spend time with other children. Others may find time to write, read, or pursue another vocation or an avocation. Many universities have committees on the status of women that study issues related to the well-being of women on campus and that make supportive recommendations, such as job sharing. Some universities have focused on employee development specifically for promising women. These institutions have invested in leadership training, support for faculty or staff travel and research, and sabbaticals to encourage leadership by women.

Some of the structural support for women in higher education evolved from the need to take the affirmative action required by the federal government. Affirmative action means taking positive steps to eliminate the effects of previous discrimination. Such steps might be the inclusion with job announcements of a statement specifically inviting women to apply, or the creation of computerized "vita" banks with the résumés of women who may be potential applicants.

Executive Order #11246 of September 24, 1965, as amended (41 C.F.R. §60-1) is the basis for affirmative action programs for most major universities and colleges. Davidson, Ginsburg, and Kay (1974) list the eight essential components of affirmative action programs:

1. A statement of affirmative action policy and a written program to implement the policy.
2. Dissemination of the affirmative action program.
3. Designation of responsibility for implementing the program.
4. A utilization analysis of female employees by department and rank. The utilization analysis compares the actual employment profile with the profile that would be expected if other variables, such as discrimination, had not intervened.

5. Establishment of goals and timetables to eliminate the deficiencies found by the utilization analysis.
6. A program of action to attain the established goals.
7. Establishing an internal audit and reporting system. The system is monitored by the affirmative action officer.
8. Support for other action programs, for example, special attention may be given to increasing the number of women in academia.

As one could predict, some institutions have been resistant to the affirmative action concept (Weitzman, 1973); others have made sincere attempts to implement the programs. Complementary to the affirmative action concept, several laws specifically prohibit discrimination on the basis of sex. Title VII of the Civil Rights Act of 1964 bars employment discrimination against women and Title IX of the Education Amendments of 1972 prohibits discrimination on the basis of sex in educational institutions.

The effectiveness of affirmative action and federal legislation has been challenged. Critics cite the declining percentages of women in some areas of education and the lack of federal enforcement. In the area of athletics alone, there has never been a finding by a federal agency of noncompliance, despite numerous complaints on record (Atkins, 1981).

However, some women have begun to use the federal laws to win major victories through consent decrees, which are settlements made before a federal judge is forced to make a decision. The Rajender consent decree at the University of Minnesota was a major victory for women in that system. Rajender was a chemistry professor at the university. When she was not offered a permanent appointment, she filed suit (Smetanka & Foley, 1982). In the seven-year struggle that followed, the litigation was expanded to include all women as a class.

When the consent decree was signed, the University of Minnesota paid Rajender $100,000 and had to pay the Sprenger law firm approximately $1.5 million and to bear the costs of processing approximately 300 additional complaints from members of the class. Total costs to the university will reach into the millions. In addition, the university must take steps to prevent further discrimination.

Other legal actions have been taken. A similar consent decree was signed at Brown University and, again, the women won not only monetary settlements for themselves, but additional commitments to affirmative action for women. The "Cornell Eleven" recently turned down a cash settlement because they want a new affirmative action plan, reforms in recruitment, hiring, and promotion criteria, and steps to improve the proportion of women who are full professors (American Educational Research Association, 1982).

As the struggle for a more positive environment for women in education continues, the need for grassroot support has become evident. During the Rajender action, workshops for litigants, attorneys, and supporters were held to provide training, information, and support. In addition, a monthly newsletter kept supporters informed of problem areas, disposition of cases, and progress (Faculty Advisory Committee for Women, 1982–83).

Students may find broad-based support in several areas. Professors, nonacademic community groups, peers, and school employees may help. Johnson (1976) documented the way a medical class dealt with sexism by professors: female and male students petitioned their faculty to refrain from sexist humor. Through their action, the students were able to shape a more positive classroom environment for both sexes.

In Madison, Wisconsin, Judge Archie Simonson was hearing a case involving the rape of a student that had occurred in a local high school. He stated that rape was a normal reaction. A group of women and men in the community petitioned to recall him from the bench, and won. He was the first judge recalled from the bench in the state of Wisconsin. Furthermore, his defeat gave notice to the judiciary that such sexist attitudes would not be tolerated in that community.

Grassroots efforts, such as judicial recall, are important for several reasons: decision-makers learn that support for blatant discrimination may be costly to them; victims of discrimination know that they are not at fault and that justice will prevail; and community action indicates that discrimination is not normative and will not be tolerated.

Because women may feel alienated or isolated in their male-dominated educational institution, many women have been actively trying to form networks. Researchers with an interest in feminist research may meet once a month to discuss the latest studies. Businesswomen in an institution may periodically invite a speaker to their luncheons to talk about a particular facet of their work. Female faculty members may have a reception for new female faculty. In addition to local groups, national networks have been established. The continuing committee for the women's agenda that emerged from the Houston convention for International Women's Year (IWY) is one group. There is also a female researchers' special-interest group that functions as part of the American Educational Research Association (AERA). Other national organizations exist. These networks function to reduce isolation and to share information.

Other networks are challenging the "old boy" system. Advocates of an "old girl" system focus primarily on employment and note how the "boys" are hired and advanced through their connections. In academia, the "boys" may be helped by being nominated for positions, collaborating with prestigious researchers who help them get grant money, being nominated to present papers or receive awards, being highly recommended for powerful chair or administrative posts, receiving editorships, and so forth. Students may be helped by working on advanced projects that give them valuable experience, co-authoring articles with major professors, getting fellowships through the recommendation process, and so forth.

Women who want to form an "old girl" system believe that women can assist each other in similar ways. When opportunities arise, they put qualified women forward. In turn, they know that if an occasion occurs, they will be put forward by those in the network and by those they helped. Implicit in the "old girl" system is a trust that women can and will assist each other.

Many women in education have come to terms with the differences among women and have recognized that a variety of strategies can be used to advance women collectively. The schisms in the past have frequently occurred between members of "action" groups and members of "establishment" groups. Each group utilizes its own methods and attracts different members.

Action groups tend to have younger, low career-status women. Frequently, the leadership pattern is voluntary or rotating. An informal structure is prevalent in these groups. Generally, action groups work outside the power structure (Klotzburger, 1973).

Klotzburger has outlined some of the goals that action groups seek:

1. Legitimizing the problem of sex discrimination by:
   a. Adopting a formal statement opposing discrimination on the basis of sex.
   b. Establishing an official committee to research and report to the association on the status of women in the profession.
   c. Allocating funds, facilities, and publications space for communication among women in the profession.
   d. Holding association meetings in places that do not practice discrimination against women.
   e. Sponsoring a series of scholarly panels/conferences on women's perspective.
2. Encouraging the recruitment of women by:
   a. Working to end discriminatory practices in the admission of women students by academic departments.
   b. Endorsing the principle of equitable stipend support regardless of sex (with allowances for child-care support).
   c. Encouraging the development of part-time programs of study.
   d. Encouraging the reevaluation of career counseling that channels women into sex-stereotyped fields.
   e. Allocating special funds for graduate education for women.
3. Eliminating obstacles to women's career development by:
   a. Encouraging the recruitment and promotion of women faculty (including an open employment system) by academic departments.
   b. Supporting the principle of equal salaries and fringe benefits for equal work.
   c. Working to eliminate antinepotism rules.
   d. Encouraging part-time faculty appointments (with

proportionate salaries, fringe benefits, promotion, and tenure) and easy transitions between full- and part-time appointments for both men and women.

e. Encouraging the establishment of child-care facilities at employing institutions and providing appropriate facilities at association meetings.
f. Endorsing nondiscriminatory maternity and parenthood leave policies by employing institutions.
g. Operating a placement service without discrimination against women in the profession.
h. Working to eliminate discriminatory practices by all fund-granting agencies; and for the equitable representation of women on all research funding review committees.
i. Instituting a system of anonymous publication reviews of manuscripts.
j. Encouraging employers to hire on the basis of professional qualification and job characteristics only—i.e., ceasing all inquiries into sex, age, family status, and family planning in job interviews.
k. Encouraging employers to cease requesting marital and parental status information on job application forms.
l. Crosslisting women on the basis of their married and single names in the association directory.
m. Assuring equitable representation of women in the formal activities of the association, including legislative councils, advisory committees, editorial boards, and convention meetings.
n. Encouraging the equitable representation of women in policy-making positions in academic departments.
o. Encouraging academic departments to make special efforts to place qualified women in top faculty and administrative ranks where current studies reveal the greatest discrimination against women.

4. Developing research and teaching on the topic of "women" by:
   a. Encouraging academic departments to establish women's studies courses.
   b. Encouraging academic departments to examine present course curricula with a view to adding materials relating to women.

c. Encouraging publishers, libraries, and academic departments to review all printed materials with a view to eliminating sex-role stereotyping.
d. Supporting, stimulating, and recognizing the legitimacy of undertaking research concerning the role and status of women in society.

5. Implementing the adopted resolutions by:
   a. Establishing a roster of qualified women for employment referral and participation in the various functions of the profession.
   b. Actively supporting Executive Order 11246, as amended by Executive Order 11375, and HEW Affirmative Action Guidelines.
   c. Appointing a staff assistant on the status of women to the association's headquarters.
   d. Establishing the official standing committee on the status of women, allocating to it sufficient research and administrative funds.
   e. Developing procedures to censure employers who fail to furnish data necessary to evaluate the status of women in their institutions.
   f. Developing sanctions to be applied in cases of proven discrimination by employers.
   g. Developing procedures to investigate individual cases of alleged sex discrimination brought to the attention of the association—e.g., establishing liaison with AAUP.
   h. Making information available on legal resources open to or providing legal counsel for women who wish to file sex discrimination complaints against their employer.
   i. Developing accreditation evaluation guidelines for academic departments and training programs with respect to sex discrimination.
   j. Distributing endorsed resolutions to academic departments and the association's full membership; and publishing them in the association's journal or newsletter.
   k. Actively supporting the amendment of federal civil rights laws to cover professional women.
   l. Developing criteria for evaluating progress in achieving equality for women.

6. Maintaining the organization by:
   a. Publishing newsletters, abstracts and research findings on women.
   b. Recruiting members.
   c. Providing facilities for the companionship of women during professional conventions.
   d. Running candidates in association elections and pressuring for the appointment of members of the group to association committees.
   e. Establishing decision-making mechanisms and governing documents.

Establishment or advisory groups are usually composed of high career-status women. Frequently, they are fact-finding bodies. They usually conduct research on the status of women, announce their findings, and sometimes recommend action. A criticism of advisory groups is that they usually deal with the past and present, but do not use their potential power to make strong recommendations for the future (Klotzburger, 1973).

Both groups have advantages and disadvantages. They can be complementary, as, for example, when action groups lobby for the implementation of the recommendations made by the establishment group.

Women who have seriously studied the change process are developing survival strategies. The students of change maintain that individuals can learn skills that will help them work within the system, produce change, and possibly even receive some of the rewards given by society. The strategies are designed for the survival of the change agent in a system. The Drug Dependence Institute at Yale University has offered guidelines for survival:

1. Decide if you are committed to working within the system. What are your alternatives?
2. Begin establishing yourself as a change agent, start with trivial changes, i.e., ask for yellow chalk instead of white. Gradually increase the significance of your requests.
3. Know that institutions are resistant to change. You will not always get the changes you want.

4. Establish a priority list. Which changes are imperative? Which can be compromised for the moment?
5. Cultivate the goodwill of your colleagues. Stretch out to them whenever possible.
6. Volunteer to serve on decision-making committees. Boring wastes of time that most committes are, remember that they have a lot of power. (Women in higher education beware. Limit the number of committee assignments you have. Be sure you have enough time left for the publish or perish game.)
7. When decisions are about to be made in committees and you realize you are going to lose, try to push a compromise that moves the decision in your direction.
8. Assess which parts of yourself you can compromise and which you cannot.
9. Try to get your department to hire someone who will be seen as more radical than you.
10. Know that if you push for change too quickly or if you cannot compromise on central issues, you will be viewed as a threat and may be forced out. If you are a change agent in a system, be sensitive to the threat you pose and try to anticipate when you might be forced out. If you realize that is happening, seek alternatives before action is taken.

Knowledge of institutional change as well as individual strategies is important for those seeking to survive in educational institutions.

Institutions go through a normal and predictable process that involves five steps toward change:

1. *Dissatisfaction.* There is a pervading sense of uneasiness. The cause for the dissatisfaction is only vaguely understood. The feeling that all is not well may begin after something novel is presented, possibly by the diffusion process.
2. *Manifest unrest.* Overt unrest is present which can be seen in emotional contagion, action, or distributed anxiety.

Actions that do occur are apt to be misdirected or undirected (i.e., riots). Actions geared for institutional change do not appear in this stage.

3. *Assessment and search for solutions.* Those who want to maintain the status quo seek to control disturbances to its predictability. Compromises are sought to reduce the threat. New patterns are searched for. Responses can go from retreatism to drastic change in the definition of the group or institutional structure.
4. *Formalization of patterns.* The possible solutions of stage three are tried in practical situations. Some are rejected and some are accepted. The ones that remain are refined and diffused. Usually the ones that survive are those that can be accepted by most people.
5. *Legitimation and institutionalization.* Society accepts the reforms. The new actions or beliefs become the norm.

An example of a change that proceeded through these five stages is woman's suffrage. It should be noted that, while five stages are listed, there are no distinct lines of demarcation. Thus, the suffrage movement passed through an entire process rather than distinct steps (Ryan, 1969). Now, few people would challenge the right to vote for women; it has become the norm and is institutionalized.

Women who seek to survive in institutions can incorporate some of the strategies and understandings that have emerged from social-change literature. The next step is to move beyond survival. As women have gained positions in institutions, some have sought to create changes to make the school more accommodating to the needs of women in general. In the process, they have become change agents and have become astute at dealing with their institutions. There are risks associated with producing change, particularly for those in the vanguard, and some women have paid dearly for their efforts. Others have survived, have advanced to positions of power, and have flourished.

Some women have achieved a measure of power and its rewards of affluence, recognition, self-esteem, and a sense of pleasure and satisfaction from the work. But women can use power differently from men. Hennig (Thurman, 1982) states that although women need to acquire the skills of leadership, "this does not mean you must renounce your vision of the world as you want it to be. Women with power do not have to act like men with power. They do not have to be co-opted." There is a growing recognition of the need to use women's power to help other women. Shalala (Thurman, 1982) asserts, "As for the woman at the top, she is no longer a single type. The 'Queen Bee' of twenty years ago—the lone woman proud of having made it on her own, demanding that younger women do the same—is an anachronism." Hennig adds that "We see those women [in senior management] bringing the pain of their own experience to the surface—becoming sensitive to the pain of the women under them. 'I have kept conscious of the difficulties,' they are saying. 'I will use my power to unravel the difficulties for my successors.' And that is the key to getting more women up there."

The vision of an ideal educational institution may vary with each woman. Some common themes emerge, however, to suggest areas of focus and possible change to create educational environments in which women can thrive.

7

Going Forth

As women have tried to move forward in education, many have developed a new consciousness of themselves and their situation. There has been an awareness that something is wrong, that only collective action can correct it, and that women can define their own goals. Women have been encouraged to develop a vision of the future for themselves and others that would provide an alternative conceptualization of society as it is being shaped now (Lerner, 1983).

Something is wrong in education. Overt indicators, such as statistical studies, show negative patterns: job segregation, declining proportions of women as level of employment increases, and student segregation by discipline. Indicators of covert processes show that women employees and students may be "cooled out" of the educational environment. Rather than being trained for and encouraged toward leadership, women may emerge from the educational process with lowered expectations and confidence in themselves.

The pervasiveness of sex discrimination in education will require collective action to counter it. Individual women may be able to carve out a niche for themselves, but the overall condition of women in education will not improve until people join together to produce the necessary changes. Since these changes are systemic, much collective work will be needed before equal rights for women becomes institutionalized.

In joining together, women will need to define and clarify their own goals for educational institutions. The inclusion of women's issues, works by women, and women's research in the curricula of each academic program is an important objective that affects how women and men view themselves in each discipline. Equal opportunity for female students and employees is a critical goal for future generations of women. Women's groups believe that educators should address peace studies, environmental concerns, care for the young and the elderly, control of nuclear power, achieving justice in the legal system, and other broad issues. Many other concerns have arisen or will arise, and women challenge educators to work with them in addressing these issues.

For physical educators, the challenge is to foster the leadership potential of women in the ranks. Physical education departments could enforce laws prohibiting discrimination, confront and overcome stereotyped attitudes, develop teacher-education modules that specifically address leadership for women in the profession, provide female role models and special support for women with leadership potential (internships, guarantees for equality in leadership opportunities, rotating leadership positions by sex), and obtain technical assistance from state or national groups (based on Geadelmann et al., 1985). In addition, the curricula of the activity professions should include research based on discussions about women's issues. Above all, women in the profession should be aware of issues concerning women in our society.

It is tantalizing to look into the future and imagine a society in which 51 percent of every decision-making body is composed of women. What national policies would be in place that affect resources allocated for education and other life-enhancing institutions? How would diversity of opinions and beliefs be negotiated to produce societal harmony? What impact would women have on the transmission of societal values? Would the austere tradition of rationality disassociated from feeling in the decision-making process continue? The questions are as limitless as the impact that women, acting collectively, could have.

As women move from the margin to the center, changes will occur in education and in society. If women exert their potential for leadership, it is exciting to contemplate what these changes might be. To make the possibilities a reality, women must look to the future and begin the process of going forth.

References

AAAA, Region IV and V Conference of the American Affirmative Action Association, [no title]. Columbus, Ohio, 1981.

Alexander, C. The physical educator, Miss or Mrs.? *DGWS Research Reports: Women in Sports*. Washington, DC: AAHPER Press, 1973, pp. 55–62.

Allport, Gordon W. *The Nature of Prejudice*. Garden City, NY: Doubleday Anchor Book, 1958, pp. 147–149.

American Educational Research Association. *AERA/SIG Research on Women in Education Newsletter*, 1982.

Ashcraft, R.J. Comparison of employment status of men and women in four-year public institutions. *JOHPER*, 1973, *44*: 60–62.

Athos, A.G. and Coffey, R.E. *Behavior in Organizations: A Multidimensional View*. Englewood Cliffs, NJ: Prentice-Hall, 1968, pp. 160–164.

Atkins, J. Interview with Women's Equity Action League. Washington, DC, 1981.

Bain, L.L. Description of the hidden curriculum in secondary physical education. *The Research Quarterly*, 1976, *47*(2): 154–159.

Belanger, C.H. and Everett, P.W. Salaries of physical education faculty in selected four-year institutions. *JOHPER*, 1973, *44*: 58–60.

Bem, S.L. The measurement of pyschological androgyny. *Journal of Consulting and Clinical Psychology*, 1974, *42*(2): 155–162.

Bernay, E. Affirmative action. *Ms.*, November 1978, pp. 87–90.

Bowers, E. and Hummel, J. *Factors related to the underrepresentation of women in vocational education administration: A literature review. Research and Development Series no. 152.* Unpublished. Columbus, OH: The National Center for Research in Vocational Education, 1979. (Available from the Center, Ohio State University, 1960 Kenny Road, Columbus, OH 43210)

Broverman, I.K., Broverman, D.M., Clarkson, F.E., Rosenkrantz, P.S., and Vogel, S.R. Sex-role stereotypes and clinical judgments of mental health. *Journal of Consulting and Clinical Psychology*, 1970, *43*(1): 1–7.

Burke, N.P. Staffing needs and dilemmas. Paper presented at the AIAW Athletic Directors Conference, Los Angeles, California, 1979.

Butler, P.E. *Self-Assertion for Women: A Guide to Becoming Androgynous*. New York: Harper and Row, 1976.

The Carnegie Commission on Higher Education. *Opportunities for Women in Higher Education*. New York: McGraw-Hill Book Company, 1973.

Clance, P.R. and Imes, S.A. The imposter phenomenon in high achieving women: Dynamics and therapeutic intervention. *Psychotherapy: Theory, Research and Practice,* Fall 1978, *15*(3): 241–247.

Condry, J. and Dyer, S. Fear of success: Attribution of cause to the victim. *Journal of Social Issues,* 1976, *32*(2): 63–79.

Coombs, R.H. *Mastering Medicine: Professional Socialization in Medical School.* New York: The Free Press, 1978.

Crawford, M. Climbing the ivy-covered walls. *Ms.,* November 1978, pp. 61–63ff.

Daly, M. *Beyond God the Father: Toward a Philosophy of Women's Liberation.* Boston: Beacon Press, 1973.

Davidson, K.M., Ginsburg, R.B., and Kay, H.H. *Sex-Based Discrimination.* St. Paul, MN: West Publishing Co., 1974, pp. 964–976.

Davies, G.H. Single physical education departments and equality for women. *JOHPER,* 1973, *44*: 62–63.

Denmark, F.L. Styles of leadership. *Psychology of Women Quarterly,* 1977, *2*(2): 99–113.

Doderer, M. Dealing with gatekeepers. In *Women As Leaders in Physical Education and Sport,* edited by M.G. Scott and M.J. Hoferek. Iowa City, IA: University of Iowa Publications Office, 1979, pp. 37–45.

Doe, J. Excerpted from: "On Campus with Women," March 1977, Association of American Colleges. *Ms.,* November 1978, p. 87.

Duquin, M.E. Institutional variables affecting women in leadership positions. In *Women As Leaders in Physical Education and Sport,* edited by M.G. Scott and M.J. Hoferek. Iowa City, IA: University of Iowa Publications Office, 1979, pp. 31–36.

Ekstrom, R.B. Problems of women researchers at three stages of professional development. Paper presented at the annual meeting of the American Psychological Association, Toronto, Canada, August 30, 1978.

Epstein, C.F. Encountering the male establishment: Sex-status limits on women's careers in the professions. *American Journal of Sociology,* 1970, *75*: 965–982.

Faculty Advisory Committee for Women Newsletter. 1982–83. (University of Minnesota).

Fallon, D. Job discrimination among doctorates in physical education. *JOHPER,* 1973, *44*: 56–57.

Felshin, J. The triple option . . . for women in sport. *Quest,* January 1974, pp. 36–40.

Fields, C.M. Appeals court rejects charge that NCAA forced women's group out of business. *The Chronicle of Higher Education,* May 30, 1984, *28*(14): 27.

41 C.F.R. §60-1.4. 1982.

Fox, M.G. *Title IX–Equality: Realty or Myth?* Paper presented at the Big Ten Physical Education Directors Conference, Chicago, Illinois, 1977.

Geadelmann, P.L., Bischoff, J., Hoferek, M.J., and McKnight, D.B. Sex equity in physical education and athletics. Chapter 17 in *Handbook for Achieving Sex Equity in Education*, edited by S. Klein. Baltimore, MD: Johns Hopkins University Press, 1985, pp. 319–337.

Gearhart, S.M. *The Wanderground: Stories of the Hill Women*. Watertown, MA: Persephone Press, 1978, pp. 118–132.

Goldberg, P. Are women prejudiced against women? *Transaction*, April 1968, pp. 28–30.

Gold Book: Directory of Physical Education in Higher Education 1982–1984. Champaign, IL: Human Kinetics Publishers, 1982, pp. 114ff.

Hacker, H.M. Women as a minority group. In *Masculine/Feminine*, edited by Roszak and Roszak, New York: Harper and Row, 1969, pp. 130–148.

Hanick, P.L. Role strain in working women: Balancing private and professional lives. Paper presented at the annual meeting of the American Alliance for Health, Physical Education, Recreation, and Dance, Boston, Massachusetts, 1981.

Heide, W.S. Feminism for a sporting future. In *Women and Sport: From Myth to Reality*, edited by C.A. Oglesby. Philadelphia: Lea and Febiger, 1978, pp. 195–202.

Helmreich, R. and Spence, J. *Sex roles and achievement.* Paper presented at NASPSPA [North American Society for the Psychology of Sport and Physical Activity], Austin, Texas, May 1976.

Hilberman, E., Konanc, J., Perez-Reyes, M., Hunter, R., Scagnelli, J., and Saunders, S. Support groups for women in medical school: A first-year program. *Journal of Medical Education*, 1975, *50*: 867–875.

Hoferek, M.J. At the crossroad: Merger or —— ? *Quest*, 1980a, *32*(1): 95–102.

———. A second chance: Equal opportunity in a deregulatory climate. Unpublished monograph.

———. Sex roles and sport: Implications of recent research. In *Equity Issues*, 1980b. (Wisconsin Sex Equity Project, 125 S. Webster Street, Madison, WI 53702)

———. Sex-role prescriptions and attitudes of physical educators. *Sex Roles: A Journal of Research*, 1982, *8*(1): 82–98.

Hoferek, M.J. and Sarnowski, A.A. Feelings of loneliness in women medical students. *Journal of Medical Education*, 1981, *56*(1): 397–403.

Holmen, M.G. and Parkhouse, B.L. Trends in the selection of coaches for female athletes: A demographic inquiry. *Research Quarterly*, March 1981, *52*(1).

Holmstrom, E.I. and Holmstrom, R.W. The plight of the woman doctoral student. *American Educational Research Journal,* Winter 1974, *11* (i): 1–17.

Horner, M. The motive to avoid success and changing aspirations of college women. In *Readings on the Psychology of Women,* edited by J.M. Barwick. New York: Harper and Row, 1972, pp. 62–67.

Hudson, J. Physical parameters used for female exclusion from law enforcement and athletics. In *Women and Sport: From Myth to Reality,* edited by C.A. Oglesby. Philadelphia: Lea and Febiger, 1978, pp. 19–57.

Illinois State Board of Education. *Equitunity in Vocational Education Administration: A Handbook for Administrators and Members of Boards of Education.* 1980. (Available from the Board, 100 North First Street, Springfield, IL 62777)

Johnson, D.G. The medical student, 1975. In *Recent Trends in Medical Education,* edited by E.F. Purcell. New York: Josiah Macy, Jr. Foundation, 1976, pp. 37–54.

Joreen [pseud.]. Trashing: The dark side of sisterhood. *Ms.,* April 1976, pp. 49–51ff.

Kaplan, S.R. Women's education: The case for single-sex college. *The Higher Education of Women,* [n.d.], pp. 53–67.

King, L.T. *Sex ratio trends in athletic leadership.* Presentation at the national conference of the American Educational Research Association, New Orleans, Louisiana, 1984.

Klotzburger, K. Political action by academic women. In *Academic Women on the Move,* edited by A.S. Rossi and R. Calderwood. New York: Russell Sage Foundation, 1973, pp. 359–391.

Laws, J.L. The psychology of tokenism: An analysis. *Sex Roles: A Journal of Research,* 1975, *9*(1): 51–67.

Lerner, G. *The effect of social change on the lives of women.* Paper presented at a symposium entitled Women's Education: The Future, Stephens College, Columbia, Missouri, February 15–18, 1983.

Loy, J.W., McPherson, B.D., and Kenyon, G. *Sport and Social Systems.* Reading, MA: Addison-Wesley, 1978, pp. 70–72.

Miller, D.C. *Handbook of Research Design and Social Measurement.* 2nd ed. New York: David McKay, 1970, p. 141.

Mischel, W. A social-learning view of sex differences in behavior. In *The Development of Sex Differences,* edited by E.E. Maccoby. 2nd ed. Stanford, CA: Stanford University Press, 1975.

Mokros, J.R., Erkut, S., and Spichiger, L. *Mentoring and Being Mentored: Sex-Related Patterns Among College Professors.* Working paper No. 68. Wellesley, MA: Wellesley College Center for Research on Women, 1981.

Morino, K.E. A preliminary investigation into the behavioral dimensions of affirmative action compliance. *Journal of Applied Psychology,* 1980, *65*(3): 346–350.

Morris, W. *The American Heritage Dictionary.* Boston: Houghton Mifflin Company, 1976, p. 1306.

Myers, L.J. *Black women in double jeopardy.* Unpublished paper. (Available from the author, 486 University Hall, 230 N. Oral Hall, Columbus, OH 43210)

National Center for Educational Statistics. *Digest of Education Statistics 1983–1984.* 0-417-806. Washington, DC: U.S. Government Printing Office, 1984.

Newman, J. and Krzystofiak, F. Self-reports versus unobtrusive measures: Balancing method variance and ethical concerns in employment discrimination research. *Journal of Applied Psychology,* 1979, *64*(1): 82–85.

Oglesby, C.A. *Feminism and sport psychology methodology.* Paper presented at NASPSPA [North American Society for the Psychology of Sport and Physical Activity], Austin, Texas, May 1976.

______. The masculinity/femininity game: Called on account of . . . In *Women and Sport: From Myth to Reality,* edited by C.A. Oglesby. Philadelphia: Lea and Febiger, 1978, pp. 75–88.

______. *Women and mentoring.* Paper presented at the annual convention of the American Alliance for Health, Physical Education, Recreation, and Dance, Boston, Massachusetts, 1981.

Olsen, N.J. and Willemsen, E.W. Fear of success—Fact or artifact? *The Journal of Psychology,* 1978, *98*: 65–70.

Parkhouse, B.L. and Williams, J.M. *Differential effects of gender and status on evaluation of coaching ability.* Manuscript under review.

Parlee, M.B. The sexes under scrutiny: From old biases to new theories. *Psychology Today,* November 1978, *12*: 62–69.

Peck, T. When women evaluate women, nothing succeeds like success: The differential effects of status upon evaluations of male and female professional ability. *Sex Roles: A Journal of Research,* 1978, *4*(2): 205–213.

Rebecca, M., Hefner, R., and Oleshansky, B. A model of sex-role transcendence. *Journal of Social Issues,* 1976, *32*(3):197–206.

Regent's Task Force on the Status of Women. *A blueprint for achievement of educational equality in the eighties.* Unpublished document. Madison, WI: University of Wisconsin, April 1981.

Richey, D. *Race and sex: Barriers minority women face in obtaining and remaining in leadership positions.* Paper presented at the annual convention of the American Alliance for Health, Physical Education,

Recreation, and Dance, Boston, Massachusetts, 1981.
Rosenthal, R. and Jacobson, L. *Pygmalion in the classroom.* New York: Holt, Rinehart and Winston, 1968, pp. vii–44.
Rulings on sex designation of physical education departments. *AAHPER Update*, 1976, *3.*
Ryan, B.F. *Social and Cultural Change.* New York: The Ronald Press Company, 1969.
Safrit, M.J. Women in research in physical education. *Quest*, 1979, *31* (2): 158–171.
Scientific Manpower Commission. *Professional Women and Minorities.* Washington, DC: The Commission, November 1978, pp. 28, 245. (Available from the Commission, 1776 Massachusetts Avenue, NW, Washington, DC 20036)
Sells, L.W. Sex differences in graduate school survival. Paper presented at the annual meeting of the American Sociological Association, New York, New York, August 18, 1973. In *Sex Discrimination in Education: A Study of Employment Practices Affecting Professional Personnel*, edited by R.D. Kane. ERIC Reports, vol. II (ED 132-744), April 1976, pp. 178– 179.
Serbin, L.A. and O'Leary, K.R. How nursery schools teach girls to shut up. *Psychology Today*, 1975, *9*(7): 57–58ff.
Smetanka, M.J. and Foley, E. The Rajender decree. *Minneapolis Tribune*, June 5, 1982.
Spears, B. Success, women, and physical education. In *Women As Leaders in Physical Education*, edited by M.G. Scott and M.J. Hoferek. Iowa City, IA: University of Iowa Publications Office, 1979, pp. 5–19.
Spiro, H.M. Visceral viewpoints: Myths and mirths—Women in medicine. *New England Journal of Medicine*, 1975, *292*: 354–356.
Stake, J.E. Educational and career confidence and motivation among female and male undergraduates. *American Educational Research Journal*, Fall 1984, *21*(3): 565–578.
Stauffer, R.W. *A Follow-up Study to: The Comparison of USMA Men and Women on Selected Physical Performance Measure . . . "Project Summertime."* West Point, NY: United States Military Academy, November 1977.
Steiner, I.D. *Group Process and Productivity.* New York: Academic Press, 1972, pp. 173–176.
Thurman, J. Power: The hang-ups, the drives, the price, and the joys. *Ms.*, December 1982, pp. 39ff.
Toffler, A. *The Third Wave.* New York: Bantam Books, 1980, p. 404.
Unger, R.K. *The student-teacher evaluation form as an instrument of sexism.* Unpublished paper. (Available from Dr. Rhoda Unger,

Montclair State College, Upper Montclair, NJ 07043)
United States Department of Labor. *The Myth and the Reality*. 0-550-115. Washington, DC: U.S. Government Printing Office, 1974, pp. 9–10.
United States Department of Labor. *20 Facts on Women Workers.* Washington, DC: U.S. Government Printing Office, 1982.
University of Wisconsin Faculty Senate Minutes, Madison, Wisconsin, March 2, 1981.
Vetter, L., Burkhardt, C., and Sechler, J. *Vocational Education Sex Equity Strategies.* Columbus, OH: The National Center for Research in Vocational Education, 1978. (Available from the Center, Ohio State University, 1960 Kenny Road, Columbus, OH 43210)
Walsh, M.R. The rediscovery of the need for a feminist medical education. *Harvard Education Review,* 1979, *49*: 447–466.
Weitzman, L.J. Affirmative action plans for eliminated sex discrimination in academe. In *Academic Women on the Move,* edited by A.S. Rossi and R. Calderwood. New York: Russell Sage Foundation, 1973, pp. 463–504.
White, M.S. Psychological and social barriers to women in science. *Science,* 1970, *170*: 413–416.
Wilmore, J.H. The female athlete. *The Journal of School Health,* 1977, pp. 227–233.
Working Women. *In defense of affirmative action: Taking the profit out of discrimination.* Paper, June 18, 1981. (Available from Working Women, 1224 Huron Road, Cleveland, OH 44115)

Organizations

American Affirmative Action Association **(AAAA)**
c/o Sheila J. Nickson
SUNY Plaza T-6
Albany, NY 12246

American Alliance for Health, Physical Education, **(AAHPERD)**
Recreation, and Dance
1900 Association Drive
Reston, VA 22091

American Association of University Professors **(AAUP)**
1012 14th Street, NW
Washington, DC 20005

American Association of University Women
2401 Virginia Avenue, NW
Washington, DC 20037

American Educational Research Association **(AERA)**
1230 Seventeenth Street, NW
Washington, DC 20036

American Educational Research Association—Women's Caucus
c/o Judith Busch
Educational Foundations Department
College of Education
University of New Mexico
Albuquerque, NM 87131

Association of Black Women in Higher Education
30 Limerick Drive
Albany, NY 12204

Association for Intercollegiate Athletics for Women **(AIAW)**
No address.

Association for Women in Psychology
c/o Joan Chrisler
666 Pelham Road, #26
New Rochelle, NY 10805

International Women's Year **(IWY)**
National Commission for the Observance of International Women's Year
Department of State
Washington, DC 20520

National Association for Girls and Women in Sport **(NAGWS)**
1900 Association Drive
Reston, VA 22091

National Association for Women Deans, Administrators, and Counselors
1325 18th Street, NW
Washington, DC 20036

National Center for Research in Vocational Education.
1960 Kenny Road
Columbus, OH

National Coalition for Women and Girls in Education
c/o National Education Association
Human and Civil Rights
1201 16th Street, NW
Washington, DC 20036

National Association of Intercollegiate Athletics **(NAIA)**
1221 Baltimore Avenue
Kansas City, MO 64105

National Collegiate Athletic Association **(NCAA)**
6299 Nall Drive
Overland Park, KS 66202

National Identification Program for the Advancement of Women
in Higher Education
Office of Women in Higher Education
American Council on Education
One Dupont Circle
Washington, D.C. 20036

National Organization of Women **(NOW)**
1401 New York Avenue, NW
Washington, DC

National Women's Law Center
1751 N Street, NW
Washington, DC 20036

National Women's Political Caucus
1275 K Street, NW
Washington, DC

National Women's Studies Association
c/o Caryn McTighe Musil
University of Maryland
College Park, MD 20742

Project on Equal Educational Rights
1413 K Street, NW, 9th Fl.
Washington, DC 20005

Project on the Status and Education of Women
Association of American Colleges
1818 R Street, NW
Washington, DC 20009

United States Olympic Committee **(USOC)**
1750 East Boulder
Colorado Springs, CO 80909

University of Michigan
Center for the Continuing Education of Women
Ann Arbor, MI

Wellesley Center for Research on Women
Wellesley College
Wellesley, MA 02181

Women's Bureau
U.S. Department of Labor
200 Constitution Avenue, NW
Washington, DC

INDEX

Action groups, 60, 61
  goals of, 61–64
Activity professions. *See* Physical education
Admission process, 24
Advancement avenues, 50
Affirmative Action, 57, 58. *See also* Equal opportunity
    challenges to the effectiveness of, 58
    eight essential components of, 57–58
American Educational Research Association (AERA), 60
Androgyny model, 7, 11, 12
Anonymous submission policy, 40
Assistantships, 25
Association for Intercollegiate Athletics for Women (AIAW), 38
Athletics. *See* Physical education

Barriers, 2, 44, 53
  external, 44, 50
  internal, 44
Bay of Pigs catastrophe, 8
Bias
  against women managers, 17
  in hiring practices, 52
  women against women, 47
Bipolar approach, 11
Brown University consent decree, 58

Career commitment, 2, 26, 28
Carnegie Commission on Higher Education, 30, 36
Civil Rights Act, Title VII, 58
Clear wish, 7
Coaches. *See also* Physical education
  percentage of female head, 37
  sex bias in the evaluation of, 48–49
Collective action, 2, 68
Confidence, 2, 28
"Cooled out" process, 27, 68
"Cornell Eleven," 59
Cornell University Medical School, 38
Cultural expectation, 10, 22
Curriculum
  absence of women's history in, 21
  covert or hidden, 1, 20, 21, 23, 29
  need to include women's issues in, 69
  overt, 20, 29
  sexist, 28

Decision making, consensual, 7–8
Demographic patterns, 1
Departments, sex-separated, 37–39
Devaluation, internal 49–50
Discrimination
  against women, 1, 23, 26, 42, 44, 49, 57, 59, 68, 69
  overt, 23
Doctorates, shortchanging of female vs. male, 32–33
Double jeopardy, 50
Double standards, 47
  and teacher evaluation, 48
  and professional status, 47, 48

Education profession, underutilization of women in, 30
Educational Amendments of 1964, Title IX, 58
Educational systems, 50, 54
  climate in, 50
  ecosystem of women in, 30–32
Equal opportunity. *See also* Affirmative action
    internalization of, 55
    systemwide approaches to, 55
Equal participation rights, 8

Establishment groups, 60, 64
Executive Order #11246, 57

Faculty
  distribution of women in, 1
  women's status in, 30–35
"Frigid sisterhood," 47
Front-loading system, 55
Full-participation model, 8

Gatekeepers, 44, 50, 51
  and students, 52
  tokens as, 46
Gate openers, 39
Gates, 44
  and hurdles, 50
"Gatherstretch," 7
Graduate degrees, earned by women, 27
Graduate students
  interaction time with faculty members, 25–26
  returning females, 26
  treatment of female vs. male, 26–27
Graduate training, 24
Grassroots efforts, effects of, 58–60
Group-think phenomenon, 8

Hiring decisions, 52
  effects of visibility on, 52
Hurdles, 44

"Imposter phenomenon," 49
Institutional environment, 2
  supportive, 56, 57
  variables fostering, 54
Institutions, changes in, 65–66
Instrumental characteristics, 10, 11
International Women's Year, 60

Job segregation, 2, 30, 68
Job sharing, 57
Juvenile delinquency, and working mothers, 17

Leader
  emotional, 4
  instrumental, 4
  formal, 3
  informal, 3
  national identification program for, 6
  13 functions of, 4
Leadership
  alternatives, 7
  androgynous, 7
  autocractic, 6
  defined, 3, 4
  democratic, 6
  development of, 5–6
  future, 9, 69
  laissez faire, 6
  messiah theory of, 2, 9
  models, 5
  personality, 5
  skills, 6
  shared, 7, 8, 9
  style, 2, 6
Learning, negative, 5

Megalomania, 9
Mentors, 2, 5, 6, 24, 25, 26, 39, 40, 41, 42, 43. *See also* Role models
  and protégé feedback system, 40
  and racial/ethnic minorities, 5–6
  female, 39–40, 42
  male vs. female, 41–42
  paucity of, 25
  sex differences in, 40
Minority groups
  need for mentors among, 5–6
  self-hatred, 44–45
  tokens, 46

National Association of Physical Education for College Women, 39
National Collegiate Athletic Association (NCAA), incorporates the AIAW, 37–38
Networks
  professional, 29
  reciprocal supportive, 29
  women's, 2, 26, 29, 60
New York Infirmary Medical College, 38
"No-problem" person, 49

Obstacles, against women, 2, 43, 44
Old-boy system, 60
Old-girl system, 60
Open system, 54, 55, 56

Participatory society, 9
Performance, malleability of, 22
Personal power, 3
Physical education
  challenges for women in, 69
  lack of research training for women in, 25
  leadership role of women in, 21, 36–37, 69
  merging of male and female departments in, 39
  minority group self-hatred in, 45
  percentage of female coaches in, 37
  rank of women in, 36
  recommendations for women in, 33
  salary of females vs. males, 35
  sex bias in the evaluation of coaches, 48–49
  surveys of professionals, 35–36
  underutilization of women in, 31–32, 37, 49
  women faculty in, 35
Physical performance, effect of training on, 22
Potential, achieving full, 2
Professional image, ideal, 28
Professional life
  first decade of, 41
  methods of advancement in, 41
Protégé, 42
Protégé system, 24, 25, 41
  breakdown of, 25

"Queen Bees," 44, 67

Rajender consent decree, 56, 58, 59
Research studies
  incomplete data about women in, 21–22
  misinterpretation of data of, 22
Revaluation, internal, 49–50
Role conflict
  external, 13–14
  internal, 10–12
Role incongruity, 10
Role models, 1, 5–6, 21, 39. *See also*, Mentors
    impact on racial/ethnic minorities, 5–6
    impact on women's achievement, 5
Role triad, 13

Salary, 1, 2, 31, 32, 34, 35, 36, 39
  differential of male vs. female, 35
Self-confidence, 68
Self-fulfilling prophecy, 23
Self-hatred, 2, 44–45
  forms of, 45
  in physical education, 45
Self-vision, 1, 5, 20, 21, 22, 23, 28, 29, 44
Sex-integrated departments, 37, 38, 39
Sexism
  grassroots efforts to combat, 58–59
  in curricula, 28
  in medical schools, 59
Sexist jokes, 5, 23
Sexual harrassment, 27
Signs of belonging, 26, 42
Simonson, Judge Archie, 59
Single-sex institutions, 28
  change to co-ed, 38
  effect on attrition rate, 28–29
  medical schools, 38
Social-learning theory, 5
Socialization process, 28
Stereotyping, sex-role, 10, 23
Strategies for change, 2, 6, 39, 42, 60
Stress
  among students, 27
  techniques to reduce, 14
Student
  actions to combat sexism, 59
  attrition, 26, 28
  differential treatment of female, 22–23
  emotional stress among, 26
  interaction time with faculty, 25, 26
  returning, 26, 56
Success, fear of, 18–19

Teacher expectations, effect on student performance, 23
Teaching assistantships, 25
Tests, psychological, 10
Third Wave, The, 9
Tokens, 46
Training
  protégé system of, 24
  research, 25
  undergraduate, 20, 23
Trashing, 45, 46

Underachievement, 19
Universal criteria system, 20, 24

Vassar College, 38

Wanderground, The, 7, 8
Women
  absentee rate among, 15
  and alternative use of power, 67
  as second-class citizens, 5
  caucuses, 29, 43
  degrees earned, 24, 27
  department chairs, 39
  discontinuous educational pattern of, 26
  distribution of in education, 30, 31
  distribution of in physical education and athletics, 31–36, 37
  expectations of, 2, 10, 14, 18, 20, 23, 68
  feelings of isolation among, 42, 60
  inaccurate information about, 14, 21–22
  internship programs for, 6
  myths about, 14, 15, 16, 17, 18, 19
  participation in the labor force, 15, 16, 17
  physiological differences of, 22
  racial minority, 50
  recruitment of, 6
  reentry students, 26, 56
  silence about, 21, 56
  socioemotional characteristics of, 10, 11
  status of, 30
  studies, 1, 56
  support groups, 56
  survival strategies for, 64–65
  turnover rate of, 16
Women's colleges. *See* Single-sex institutions
Women's Liberation Movement, 6
Workshops, in-service, 6

Yale University Drug Dependence Institute, 64